The SHORTER Guide to Building a Better Business

JOHN SHORTER

Published by Filament Publishing Ltd
16, Croydon Road, Beddington,
Croydon Surrey, CR0 4PA   UK
www.filamentpublishing.com
info@filamentpublishing.com
+44(0)20 8688 2598

The Shorter Guide to Building a Better Business
by John S D Shorter

ISBN 978-1-913623-97-5
© 2022 John Shorter

All rights reserved
No portion of this work may be copied without the prior written permission of the publishers

The right to be identified as the author of this work has been asserted by John S D Shorter in accordance with the Designs and Copyrights Act 1988

Design: Andy Batchelor
Illustration: Andy Hunt, Totally Barking, Launceston, Cornwall

Originally produced by Aurora Print and Design Ltd

Printed in the UK from responsible sources

WARNING

Be warned, this delightful book is bursting with amusing stuff which will bring a smile to your face and it will prove to be difficult to put down once you have started it. However, the underlying intention of the book is not purely to amuse but also to draw serious conclusions and to share important lessons from the experiences so eloquently described.

This book is relevant to ANY entrepreneur who is determined to succeed in a chosen field. The many lessons which John Shorter learned over the decades as a financial adviser can be equally applied to any other trade or profession.

The secret of success in business, any business, is to keep doing the right thing by the clients over and over. No one ever said it was easy but this book contains so many nuggets of wisdom which will help."

Paul Joslyn
Past President of the Life Assurance Association
Chartered Financial Planner (retired)

What People are Saying

Tony GORDON
Past President of the Life Insurance Association and of The Million Dollar Round Table

John Shorter has spent his working life as a financial adviser, a very successful one. His book is a light hearted look at his journey to success, how important lessons were learned. Lessons which helped him build great relationships with his clients which have stood the test of time. This book should certainly be read by financial advisers but also by all who believe that good business hinges on good relationships.

Justin URQUHART STEWART
Co-Founder of Seven Investment Management LLP & Chairman of Regionally

This lovely little book from a great success contains so many great lessons for a great career. These are wise words, well told. They are all gold for budding entrepreneurs. In my view, this book is an essential read for anyone seeking success in their particular field.

Richard BATEMAN
Director Bateman Financial Management

John is the most naturally gifted adviser I have ever met and he is someone you instantly know you can trust. He always has time for other people and is a fantastic listener with wonderful communication skills. If he wasn't retired, I would have him advising me on my financial affairs.

Bhupinder ANAND
Managing Director of Anand Financial Architecture and twice awarded "IFA of the Year"

The word 'genius' is reserved for only a select few people... but it is a term which describes my friend John Shorter perfectly. He always amazes me with his unique ability to simplify complex matters and to get to the core of an issue. His character and style is endearing and he has helped so many people improve not just their finances, but also their lives. His story and experiences will inspire and amuse all readers of this delightful book.

Ted DWYER
Founder Director of City Life, Cork (Established 1971)

I first met John when we were each asked to speak at an LIA Conference in Birmingham. We both shared a love of being financial advisers and also of salmon fishing. We also enjoyed learning from the best in the world by attending the Million Dollar Round Table Meetings. John has been a great friend and mentor. Thank you and good luck with what I know will be a wonderful book.

Danby BLOCH
Chairman, City IFAs Helm Godfrey Partners Ltd

Over the years that I knew John, I discovered someone who was able to summarise into a few clear words ideas that most people regarded as impenetrable and even dull. It is that, I think, that was much of the secret of his success.

Chris LEACH
Managing Director of Chris Leach & Associates Ltd. Past President of the Life Insurance Association

What can I say about John? Perfectly turned out, always focused, creative, articulate, thoughtful, clever.... I am proud to have known John for many years. A superb IFA in his time, always there with a solution no matter what the problem. New IFAs coming through could learn a lot from him.

Brendan GLENNON
Retired CEO of Life Insurance Association Ireland

John Shorter is well-known and a highly-respected adviser throughout his long career. He was a very early member of The Life Insurance Association (LIA), who conscientiously collected almost every monthly issue of the LIA's "Prospect" magazine. To share knowledge with colleagues, he generously donated his entire collection to enable this wonderful resource to be made available for posterity.

John EARDLEY
Independent Financial Planner at Parsonage Limited

I met John at a business conference in the mid-1990s and we became good friends and corresponded regularly. He totally inspired me to greater heights with his professionalism and his brilliant use of the English language in order to make complex financial matters understandable. A top man at his craft.

Len SAMSON
Principal and Director of Strategy of Premview Properties Ltd

I have known John for 50+ years during which time we were both members of Toptrak. Fellow members and I were always keen to see John's ideas. He possesses an extraordinary ability to simplify the most complex issues for the benefit of the public. Thanks for all your sharing, John.

Robert SHERIDAN
Ex-Director Abbey Life

I recruited John in the 70s. He was always punctual, smart and businesslike. John conscientiously followed the disciplines for success. He always took a long-term view of developing his business and tailored the right plan within the client's budget. We enjoyed a mutually rewarding relationship and are friends to this day.

Simon GIBSON
Chief Investment Officer Mattioli Woods plc

When it was unfashionable (but safe) John was a super-spreader - his "virus" was good ideas, positivity and a willingness to give a leg up if he could. I learned much from you, John. Thank you.

Mark HOLLAND
Senior Partner, St James's Place Wealth Management

I so enjoyed working with John and the team and I am glad I persevered in getting an interview to see him in 1993. My current success owes so much to what he taught me and he will always remain my most inspiring mentor. I regard John as a true friend.

ABOUT THE AUTHOR

John Shorter was educated at Brentwood Public School in the fifties. At the end of his education, he was keen to escape and get into the world of working and at age 16 joined a firm of Lloyd's Insurance Brokers in The City just like his father and grandfather had before him. John's work involved helping overseas Agents to get risks placed in the Lloyd's market.

Whilst he always enjoyed his work, he felt that he wanted to exert a more direct influence on people's lives. He left The City and headed for the West End where he sold the products of a couple of major Life Insurance Companies over the next few years. Here he felt a lot more at home because he was dealing directly with members of the public.

After a few years, however, he started to think that, if he was genuinely to offer his clients the very best products available in the whole market, he should become totally independent. Thus began a thirty-two year career as an Independent Financial Adviser where he created and built a substantial business which was eventually sold in 2012. He and his wife Vivienne, have three boys all of whom have matured into successful entrepreneurs in their own rights. His hobbies include collecting antiques, game fishing, woodturning and listening to jazz and classical music.

*This book is dedicated to my three sons,
Giles, Jerome and Alexander in whom I have great pride.*

Contents

WHAT PEOPLE ARE SAYING	4
ACKNOWLEDGEMENTS	12
INTRODUCTION	14
HOW IT ALL STARTED	17
A PERSONAL ENCOUNTER WHICH CHANGED MY LIFE	23
A LUCKY MEETING	27
FROM LAMPSHADES GROW CLIENTS	33
A VERY DODGY START	39
SATURDAY IN ISLINGTON	45
AN UNFORTUNATE MISUNDERSTANDING	51
IN THE NICK OF TIME	55
PISS-CATORIAL PURSUITS	61
SELLING AND MIS-SELLING	65
POOR PROSPECTS	73
THE RIGHT CHOICE	79
A FOOL AND HIS MONEY	93
POOR TIMEKEEPING	97
MIXED BLESSINGS	103
TURNOVER IS VANITY, PROFIT IS SANITY	109
RICH IS BETTER	115
NEW BLOOD	121
SOME POINTS TO PONDER	125
KEEPING IT SIMPLE	127
TOPTRAK	131
THE LIFE INSURANCE ASSOCIATION & MDRT	135
FROM BEGINNING TO END	139
SOME USEFUL IDEAS	151
THE CONCLUSION	173

Acknowledgements

Where do I start? I am grateful to so many people for having encouraged or empowered me to write this little book.

Firstly, and most importantly, I want to pay homage to the patience and generosity of my wonderful wife of 45 summers, Vivienne. It was she who gave me the courage to write this in the first place. It was also she who showed such genuine interest and offered such valuable suggestions when I asked her for the umpteenth time to listen to my drafts. As usual, when she says with great sincerity, "You can do it", I find that I invariably can. Most of us can achieve all sorts of things so long as someone whom we respect says that we can. I have always been so lucky in that she has never once failed to encourage, cajole or give me a helping hand whenever required.

I also wish to thank all those people who encouraged me during the very early days of my career to be persistent, respectful, patient and honest in all my dealings with the public. People like Robert Sheridan, the Branch Manager of Abbey Life where I cut my teeth back in the 1970s. Without his unwavering faith in me as a budding adviser, I probably would have drifted off and done something else not as worthwhile and less fulfilling. Then, this book would certainly never have seen the light of day.

Then there are all those dedicated fellow professionals who have selflessly offered me their advice or ideas or those who have given me inspiration or motivation when needed.

Special thanks are due to all those who offered suggestions or recommendations over the contents of this book including Tony Gordon, Bhupinder Anand, Ted Dwyer, Christine Leach, Brendan Glennon, Lee Clarke, Richard Bateman, Simon Gibson, Clyde Young, John Eardley, Mark Holland and many others. I also wish to express my gratitude to Andy Batchelor for his skill in putting this book together and, of course, to Andy Hunt for his wonderful illustrations.

"One of my earliest memories is of sitting on my mother's lap with an atlas".

Introduction

I've been much blessed in that I have been engaged in a job which I enjoyed so much for so long. I was an early member of the "Thank God it's Monday Club". So many lovely and amusing things have happened to me in my career that I want to write them down in case I forget them. Of course, it hasn't all been plain sailing. There have been desperate times when I have been tempted to think that no kind of success would ever materialise. However, I am a salmon fisherman and so it always seems that another cast might just do it.

One of the first questions they ask you when you say you want to write a book is: "What is your market? Who do you envisage will be reading your book? To be honest, I believe it will be relevant and of interest to anyone who decides to go it alone in business, I mean ANY business. As it happens, my particular chosen field happened to be financial services but the problems and challenges which I encountered on my journey would have been very much the same whatever trade or profession I might have chosen. You might have noticed that I have dedicated this book to my three sons Giles, Jerome and Alexander. The particular methods of earning a living which they have each selected could not be more diverse. Giles is an Architect, Jerome a furniture designer/upholsterer and Alexander, a property developer. They are each doing very well. Nothing gives me greater pleasure nowadays than to have a chat over a pint with each of my sons about how business is going. I have noticed, every time, that exactly the same subjects crop up in our conversations which I personally grappled with when I was growing my business. How do I get more or better quality staff? How can I aim 'up market'? How can I attract better clients or customers? How can I keep on top of new legislation or regulations? How can I keep abreast of the latest technology? How can I improve cashflow? These are all typical queries occurring to any conscientious entrepreneur who is intent upon succeeding in his chosen field. There were times during the formative years of my little enterprise when the daily problems and challenges which life chucked at me threatened to destroy my resolve. However, if one has responsibilities or obligations to other people or loved ones, you cannot allow any negative thoughts to enter the head, can you?

For those who are just thinking of starting a business of some sort, the most compelling question, of course, is, " When shall I do it?". Now, there's an interesting question. There are those who would say that, if some sort of dramatic social or political event has just occurred, or is just about to occur, it would obviously be better to wait until things have died down. As I write this, the COVID-19 disaster which has devastated the entire globe provides a wonderful excuse for the procrastinators. "Let's just delay things until the pandemic is over" I hear them say. The trouble is that these cataclysmic events keep relentlessly recurring throughout the years. In 1980, when I started my enterprise, there was a change of President in the USA, Alexandra Palace in London was destroyed by fire, John Lennon was assassinated in New York, my wife Vivienne was pregnant with our first son and we were living in a caravan in the grounds of a Kent farmhouse which needed complete renovation before we could live in it. All excellent reasons for NOT starting a business at that time. Once the business was under way, in subsequent years we had Chernobyl (1986), the Black Monday Crash (1987), the Gulf War (1991), Black Wednesday (1992), the Terrorist attack on America (2001) and so on throughout the years. This type of event will of course continue occurring periodically throughout history. Of that you can be certain. Given that these things are bound to crop up, it seems a futile exercise to try to time the commencement of your new enterprise so that it falls just after a negative influence on the world fades away. If history is anything to go by (and I would suggest that it is), another cataclysmic event is probably just around the corner! The person with real entrepreneurial spirit girds his/her loins and just starts the enterprise anyway. Jumping into swimming pools spring to mind.

Going back to 1980, any thoughts I may have had of giving up were immediately banished. They had to be. The career I had chosen was the only one which would provide the wherewithal for my family to exist. The business had to survive and thrive. What was needed was a persistent nature and plenty of determination.

Consider three of the world's best known successful business people. Andrew Carnegie, Oprah Winfrey and our own Sir Richard Branson. Carnegie was born in Scotland in a typical weaver's cottage with one main room. He earned $1.20 per week as a bobbin boy in a cotton mill. He amassed $309 billion. Oprah Winfrey could hardly have entered the world in poorer conditions. She's now the highest paid figure in show business. Sir Richard Branson started his business career selling Christmas trees and budgerigars. He failed at it. He has dyslexia and yet according to Forbes (March 2021), they estimate his net worth at $5.2 billion. I would suggest that these three beacons of success all had two attributes in common. Persistency and determination. One of my earliest memories is of sitting on my mother's lap with an atlas and asking her if it may be possible to place oneself somewhere near Panama and literally transfer the Atlantic Ocean into the Pacific one spoonful at a time. At age 5 or so, it seemed to me to be perfectly feasible to do so given lots of time and bags of determination. I think that this early query on my part exemplified a part of my character which I have carried through my life so far. In other words, anything is possible so long as there is enough time and determination in evidence. This little book is designed to encourage anyone who believes in themselves and their abilities to enjoy and flourish in their chosen careers. It may take a long time, it may take a superhuman amount of resolve but it stands to reason that anyone can make a go of it, "One Spoonful at a Time".

How it all Started

*Starting work in The City - Leaving home and
working in a laundry - A lucky break
- Exploring the world with the Merchant Navy
- Back to the parental home and The City once more
- A grave disappointment caused a change of direction
- My life changed as I joined the life assurance industry.*

On leaving Brentwood Public School in Essex, an experience that I had enthusiastically looked forward to for each of the final years of my education, I joined a firm of Lloyd's Insurance Brokers in Clements Lane in The City. I had always aspired to be "Something in the City" for as long as I could recall. My father had worked all his life in a firm of Brokers in Lloyd's Avenue alongside his father who had started the enterprise, probably in the late 1890s (I really must research that some day). The firm of Eberli Shorter was well-established in The City and, of course, bore my surname. It would have been easy to join the family firm but I was always fearful of being branded the boss' son, so I insisted I went it alone, so to speak. I seem to recall that my father knew someone in the old firm of Morice Tozer & Beck and arranged for me to be interviewed by a senior man within the Personnel Department. In those days, the early sixties, jobs were very much easier to come by than today and it was accordingly with little surprise that I received a letter through the post a few days later asking me to become a member of staff on a salary of £500 a year. Naturally, I jumped at the chance to be given the opportunity to start on the road to riches at that high level! My job in the Non-Marine Claims Department initially involved manually scanning all the morning post and ensuring that each letter was distributed to the appropriate person who was dealing with that matter. There were six other people in the department if I recall correctly. In time, I was entrusted with slightly more important tasks such as filing and, on occasion, even popping out to buy a sandwich for my boss's lunch. I should say that, whatever I was asked to do, I did with great enthusiasm and a willingness to please. I enjoyed working with my colleagues and they seemed to like me too. I remained in that department for about two years by which time my annual salary had risen by 20% to £600. Whilst my time at work gave me nothing but pleasure each day, the same could not be said of my life at home with my parents. I was, after all, very wilful and had been going through a very difficult adolescence. I was so unhappy that one day, in a fit of pique, I grabbed the family car and tearfully drove off through the night to God-knows-where. I ended up in Hereford of all places. I had been subconscientiously drawn to that place because an acquaintance of mine from Brentwood had settled there some months before. I looked him up and was invited to go back to his squalid flat to meet his friends who had also drifted to Hereford for a new life.

As my departure from the parental home had been somewhat hurried and unplanned , I had very little money with me and indeed had very little money – period. Perhaps a Post Office account and some residue in the bank from the previous month's salary. My new friends in the flat had asked me if I would care to chip in with them and enjoy the security of having a roof over my head. This seemed to me to be a wonderful offer and I gratefully accepted their invitation to join with them. My share of the rent I was told would be £5 per week. It was only after a few weeks that I learned I was not only paying my share but theirs as well! This was a cruel early lesson and it taught me to be much less trusting of others in my future dealings. After a few weeks, my savings had completely run out and I was obliged to take a job in a laundry to make ends meet. Most of the hotels in the area used the services of this particular laundry and my job was to push the heavy trolleys full of wet sheets and blankets from one end of the laundry building to the other. What a transformation that was for me – City slicker to junior dogsbody in a laundry!

Following the deception my flatmates had played on me, I felt very unsettled and ready to move on elsewhere. It was while I was contemplating that dilemma that my father wrote to me (I had kept up some awkward and spasmodic correspondence during my absence from the parental home) and asked me if I'd care to consider a career in the Merchant Navy. This was a novel thought for me and, in my then predicament, one which I was certainly prepared to entertain. My father knew someone who was quite important in Ellerman Lines whose Head Office was in Camomile Street opposite Liverpool Street Station.

A couple of weeks later, I was interviewed and accepted and told to kit myself out at Gieves and Hawkes in Savile Row. This I duly did (thanks again Dad) and then I was bound for Cape Town on the good ship "City of Exeter".

Looking back on it, I am very lucky and grateful that my father helped me to meet the right people (twice). I have borne my own good fortune very much in mind when dealing with my own three boys' careers.

I remained with Ellerman Lines for four years and was lucky enough to have been around the world quite extensively. I worked in the Purser's Department and progressed from Ship's Writer (one step up from a cockroach) to Second

Steward. I was told that, on my next trip, I would probably be promoted to Assistant Purser and then it would be a short step to "having my own ship" which meant being a Purser/Chief Steward. Although I had enjoyed my experience by then, I had no desire to live a life of excess, remain single (although not necessarily celibate) and spend the next twenty years ageing forty years as seemed to be so common with my senior colleagues in the Purser's Department.

It was therefore with mixed emotions that I handed in my notice and left the Merchant Service. Unknown to me at the time, I had seen the best years anyway as the mighty Merchant Fleet became a shadow of its former self over the decades which followed thanks mainly to the burgeoning containerisation of cargo. Following my final trip therefore I found myself out of work and living temporarily back with my mother and father. Actually, my four-year absence had seen me mature and I got on a lot better, and appreciated, my parents a great deal more than before.

I made a decision to go back to the City and applied to re-join Messrs Morice, Tozer and Beck. It would have been better for me if I had not done that. I was surrounded by smallminded individuals who were still in the same ruts. Of course, I had changed considerably since I had been away. I had had the corners knocked off me and had matured beyond my age in those four years. I recall passing a Director in the corridor and hearing him casually say, "Hello Shorter, haven't seen you recently".

My second stint at Morice Tozer and Beck was in the Non-Marine Department which was responsible for placing new risks in the Lloyd's market. These opportunities for new business came from our European agents – mainly in Switzerland, Germany and France. It was interesting work and I enjoyed using my schoolboy French and more sketchy German to translate the letters which came in each day. My job was to interpret accurately the requirements of the clients and then to design the appropriate wording on a "slip" for presentation to Lloyd's Underwriters. It was very varied work which involved great care with words. Just my style. I had a small team of brokers whose job it was to see the Underwriters with a view to placing the risks. In time, I was given the opportunity to go into Lloyd's to place the risks myself. I must say, I found this very rewarding. Taking the job through from translation of the initial letter to design of the "slip", presentation to the Underwriters and then finally writing to the Agent to let him know the terms upon which the policy would be written. This was responsible work and I enjoyed the challenge enormously. As my responsibilities within the department grew, so did my youthful zeal for learning more about the somewhat complicated area of Contractors' All Risks Insurance. These were multimillion pound building contracts, mainly on the Continent, where our Agents sometimes managed to get an opportunity to quote for the insurance. The nature of this type of business more often than not, involved vast Sums Insured and accordingly very high premiums and therefore high Broker Commission. To learn about the subject, I felt the starting point was for me to read the many files of previously-placed Contracts. At the back of our office was a range of filing cabinets which contained nothing but these cases. Some of the files were extremely thick as they had taken years to conclude. Each evening, I would take a number of these files home with me. I would read them on the train and took great pains to ensure that the correspondence was all placed in strict date order and that it all made sense from cover to cover. When at home, I took great pleasure to replace all the folders which had become worn or torn. This gargantuan exercise took a number of months to conclude. No one told me to do this stuff – it was self-inflicted and was done to satisfy my hunger to learn about this fascinating area of insurance. As time went by, I felt I could finish it by the end of December if I made a concerted effort. By the time we broke for the Christmas recess, I still had about 30 or 40 files to go. I knew I would never get the job done by my self-imposed deadline unless I took them all home and dealt with them over my Christmas holiday. I borrowed an ancient trunk from the caretaker of the building and dragged it, bursting with files, along Bishopsgate to Liverpool Street Station. The job was completed by Christmas Eve.

When I came back to the office after Christmas, I busied myself placing all the newly-refurbished files back into a designated filing-cabinet at the back of the office. I took some holiday in February and went away for a couple of weeks. On my return to the office, I was horrified to find that the filing-cabinet was missing. It transpired that our Director (a man for whom none of us held any respect or affection), had taken it upon himself to have hundreds of files, including my precious Contractors' All Risks files, incinerated to make things neater! This was the beginning of the end for me and, once more, I found myself thinking of moving on to something else.

One of the Brokers I had in the team at my disposal had left Morice Tozer a year earlier and had joined a life assurance company as a salesman (then called "An Agent"). He seemed to be making much more money as a salesman and I was sufficiently intrigued to go for an interview where I was enthusiastically welcomed into the Central London Branch a few weeks later.

A Personal Encounter Which Changed my Life

*A meeting which shaped my future thinking
- The slow, deliberate technique to describing complicated issues
- There's plenty of business on one's own doorstep.*

In about 1972, I attended a Business Seminar along with about 2000 other ambitious and enthusiastic young business people. The main speaker was someone I had certainly not heard of at the time but who has actually shaped my thinking ever since. His name was Ben Feldman and he had the distinction of being fêted as the world's most successful Life Assurance salesman. The title still applies though he died over 20 years ago. This man thought in millions while most of his audience were probably thinking in hundreds.

He was a man of small though stocky stature. His strip of grey hair fringed a shiny scalp. Altogether a most unprepossessing and ordinary-looking man. When he started to speak on that stage, however, I knew that this was going to be something special. He spoke with a slow American and very deliberate style which somehow caused one to listen very intently, hungry for the next beautifully-expressed concept. One had the impression that even the most complex idea would be so skilfully expressed that even the dimmest of individuals would readily grasp the meaning. I also had the distinct feeling that Ben would never move onto the next sentence until he was certain beyond doubt that the person he was talking to had fully understood the previous sentence. That was, most probably, one of the attributes which made him such an extraordinary success.

Ben Feldman had been born in the early 20s in a small town called East Liverpool in Ohio. Whilst his contemporaries in the professional selling business were dashing all over the States chasing opportunities, he remained in the same town and simply concentrated on seeing as many business owners and family men as he could to sell his wares. The total population of East Liverpool was less than 10,000 and he reasonably felt that this was quite enough people with whom to do business. Just think of the time and petrol he saved!

The valuable nuggets of wisdom flowed thick and slow that day. Ben methodically came out with one idea after another that had me reaching for my notepad lest one escaped. One of the expressions he used that day really resonated with me. He said, "Either Man makes money or money makes money". To emphasise this, he repeated the words again. "Either Man makes money or money makes money". He was extolling the magical value of life assurance and getting across, in a clear way that everyone can understand, the fact that, if a man dies and therefore ceases to produce income for his family, a chunk of money created by a life assurance policy on his life will continue to create an income for them thus avoiding the financial catastrophe that could otherwise befall his widow and children. The simplicity of the words he used subliminally drew a picture in my sub-conscious mind of a family man being removed only to be magically replaced by a pile of money from which, when deposited somewhere, a replacement income would save the family from financial ruin. Powerful stuff.

It occurred to me that the same expression would be just as apt to describe the situation which arises when a man retires. When he decides to stop work, a lump sum of money (i.e. a pension pot) could be used to produce an income for him and his family into the years ahead.

I learned from Ben Feldman how to speak more slowly and deliberately when explaining new concepts to an interested listener. Too many people gabble away at too fast a speed, totally failing to observe the signs clearly exhibited by the listener that they are confused or simply unable to understand. Many listeners are too polite to interrupt the flow or too embarrassed to admit that they have failed to comprehend. They often continue to listen in the hope that all will come clear to them soon. The longer the speaker continues, however, the less likely that it will ever make sense to the listener. It takes courage to admit that it's all "Double Dutch" or that there's no point in carrying on with the meeting. The more likely outcome is that the speaker will go on talking and the listener will go on listening until the bitter end. Then the dreaded expression, "Well, you've given me a lot to think about" will end the meeting which might by then have lasted an hour or two. A total waste of time for both parties.

On the basis that no one buys anything that they don't understand, (whether an idea or a product) it is in the interest of both parties to proceed slowly to ensure that each part of the presentation has been digested and fully understood before moving on to the next one. An empathetic and staged approach should be employed with regular enquiries made as to whether each progressive point has been accepted and fully understood. The repeating of pivotal words or expressions is a useful technique (a method which was often used by Ben Feldman).

If, on enquiry, each point has been accepted and agreed, the end result should be to buy (in the case of a product) or to unequivocally accept (in the case of a theory or concept). Someone a lot wiser than me once said, "If you can't fault the assumptions, you must accept the conclusion".

Of course, a financial services practitioner is likely to encounter a wide range of prospective clients, some being better informed or quicker-on-the-uptake than others. The speed of delivery must also be varied accordingly. There is a fine distinction between informing slowly and "teaching grandmother to suck eggs". Therein lies the skill of successful presenting. The listener's telltale signs of comprehension, genuine interest or total boredom, if heeded, will provide ongoing guidance.

— CHAPTER ONE —

A Lucky Meeting

A trip to a Spanish supermarket - A business opportunity arises - A hasty fax to the office - leading to a loyal client.

When our three boys were all quite little, my wife, Vivienne and I took them to the south of Spain for a beach holiday in the sun. At that time, I have to admit, that family holidays fell into the category of unwelcome interruptions to my business life. My work/life balance was completely to cock. I have now totally changed my view and genuinely can't wait for my next foreign adventure.

On waking on that first morning I resolved to stay in the apartment to read that month's issue of Money Management magazine. I was generally so busy that spare time for such luxuries seldom made itself available. No sooner had I settled down on the sofa after breakfast when Vivienne asked me to help to prepare the children's paraphernalia for a nice trip down to the beach for a day of infantile fun. The disappointment must have shown on my face and she suggested that, as I obviously found playing with my own boys so unattractive, I may care to do some food-shopping instead! Thus, I was told to go to the local supermarket with baby in the pushchair for company. As he was still taking his post-breakfast nap, I felt that there was still a distinct possibility that I would be able to read my Money Management in peace after all. A short stroll to the supermarket and I stopped off for a coffee and pastry in the cafe? before embarking upon the food-shopping. Whilst reading my magazine, I became aware of the elderly gentleman whose table I was sharing. He was staring at me and seemed to be plucking up courage to engage me in conversation. I caught his eye and he asked me in a gentle North London accent if I was an Accountant. He had noticed the cover of my magazine and had jumped to an understandable conclusion. I said that I was not an Accountant but an Independent Financial Adviser. This seemed to please him as, he explained, that he had only recently sold his successful business and had a considerable amount of money to invest. It appears that his Accountant had told him sensibly to seek advice from an Independent Financial Adviser on how best to invest his new fortune to produce a tax-efficient income for the rest of his life. It was blissful serendipity that had put us together. He then asked me for my name and address so he could make contact with me when we were both back in England. I said that I had a better idea. "Give me your address and I'll drop you a line with some details on my Company". He did so and then left. Thanking my lucky stars that the opportunity to do business had so unexpectedly arisen, I then immediately quit the supermarket and pushed the buggy down the road to a swanky hotel where I drafted a letter to my potential client. Luckily for me, baby remained asleep throughout this entire process. I then faxed my scribblings to my secretary back in Eastbourne and instructed her to ensure that the letter together with its contents were posted that very day to my prospective client in Essex. I remembered that he had said he was due to fly back to Gatwick within a couple of days and I imagined how gobsmacked he would be to find my letter on his mat a day or two after his return. I made telephone contact with him on my return and during our subsequent meeting he said that he **had** been very pleasantly surprised to find my letter in the pile on his welcome mat. In the many years during which he remained a substantial client of mine, he often mentioned how I had differentiated myself from so many others who promised the earth and yet seldom, if ever, delivered

The commission which I earned from that lucky meeting paid for the entire holiday and a couple more besides.

"*He was staring at me and seemed to be plucking up courage to engage me in conversation*".

This little tale demonstrates that an alertness to opportunity coupled with some imaginative action can result in a very desirable outcome. Of course, some would say that family holidays present the business person with the opportunity to unwind and totally relax. This, they say, is the perfect chance to avoid anything that smacks of "opportunity". The practical reality, however, is that I earned enough from that chance encounter to pay not only for that holiday but a couple more besides. More importantly, the gentleman who had a need (investment advice) received it and enjoyed the benefit of substantial growth of his investment coupled with tax-efficient income over many years.

It never ceases to surprise me when I am reflecting upon the origin of many happy client relationships how many started in this way. A chance encounter initiates a conversation which leads to the uncovering of a need which can be satisfied by a product or maybe the cobbling together of a couple or more products. I once started up a conversation with a chap in an adjoining urinal which led to a savings plan - but that's another story!

Such is the variety of problems which can be solved by the financial adviser that opportunities to help are around us all the time. All that is necessary is to recognise the signs, a deep intake of breath and a summonsing of courage to engage in a conversation. Instinct will do the rest and those opportunities to help will nearly always present themselves naturally.

As always, if the mind focuses on "How can I help?" rather than "What's in it for me?" You are unlikely to meet opposition. Moreover, you are likely to enjoy a conversation which will lead to a mutually beneficial relationship.

I've spent a lifetime selling products which cannot be seen, touched or felt (i.e.intangibles) where the benefits usually only become available on death, illness or retirement - often in many decades' time.

Whilst, of course, certain attributes are clearly required in the sale of items which offer an immediate benefit or instant gratification (as in the case of a bespoke kitchen, an exotic holiday or a second home), intangibles require a very different set of skills.

— CHAPTER TWO —

From Lampshades Grow Clients!

*Sheer frustration leads to a shopping expedition
- A chance encounter leads to five sales.*

I'd been told by my mentors that every "No" brings me closer to the next "Yes". However, sometimes, after an inordinately large number of "Nos" it just seems downright unfair. More than a person can be expected to bear. One afternoon, after a mammoth session on the telephone, I was really suffering in the offices of Abbey Life at Oxford Circus where I was just trying to make an honest living. I stopped what I was doing and recalled that someone with more experience than me had suggested that, at such times, I should give myself a break and do something totally different - something pleasurable, just until the wave of pessimism passes.

After a moment, I decided that a little retail therapy might provide a suitable diversion. I therefore took a walk down Oxford Street towards Marble Arch. Upon reaching John Lewis, I remembered that I was in the market for a pair of lampshades. I therefore paid a visit to the lighting department. As soon as I stopped to look at a particular shade, an over-enthusiastic middle-aged male assistant who I judged to be Caribbean in origin asked me if I wanted that shade but in another colour. I politely said that I was just looking and he left me alone. Two minutes later, he was at my elbow once more. Was that the right size shade? Was it a suitable shape? Would I like to look at something a bit larger? We have it in other colours etc. etc. The questions and comments kept coming and I was beginning to find his behaviour quite trying. Remembering what I had been taught about selling things, I recognised and appreciated his zeal but deplored the unsubtle way he was displaying it. I assured him that I would come to him if and when I had some questions for him to answer. Again, he retreated but only for an instant. As it happens, at that moment, I spotted a pair of lampshades which I felt would probably do the trick. I reached up onto the shelf and a helping hand from "you know who" was immediately there to assist. I was asked whether I would prefer to pay by cash or cheque (more senior readers may recall cheques!). I told my friend that I would prefer to pay by cheque and he asked me if I had a cheque guarantee card to support it. A little fed up with him by this time, I said, rather tetchily, that I did, of course, have a cheque card. He wrapped the

"He introduced me to his two daughters, his two sons and his wife".

shades and then asked me for the cheque and cheque card. I wrote out the cheque and then, to my embarrassment, found that I must have left the all-important cheque card back on my desk in the office. Concerned that he might see the sale melt before his eyes, he asked me if I had some form of identification on my person. I then proffered my Abbey Life business card. He studied it for a moment and then said, "Do you by any chance arrange long-term savings plans?". Suddenly, I saw the gentleman in a totally fresh light. I replied that I did indeed arrange such plans and asked him if I could be of any help.

The following weekend, I met him in his house and he introduced me to his two daughters, his two sons and his wife. They each proceeded to take out regular premium savings plans there and then. I cannot recall ever having made five sales at one sitting – before or since.

As I say, what a thoroughly charming and delightful man he was! Salt of the earth.

There are occasions when a little break from whatever one is doing really does pay dividends. This is especially the case when all the cards seem to be stacked against you. A change of scene certainly worked well for me that day in 1975. A temporarily mislaid cheque guarantee card caused me to offer my business card as an alternative. The sight of it jogged the memory of the lampshade salesman and as a result five savings plans were bought. It just goes to show that everyone is in the market for something at some time.

Just take a moment to consider what you may be in the market for right now. It could be that you need to have double-glazing installed, maybe a new car or you need to organise a family holiday. Whatever it is, you haven't bothered to organise the transaction yet even though it's within your current budget. It could be that the purchase of the item in question isn't deemed urgent enough in your own mind. Your brain could well be telling you that there's no hurry - next week will do. It's so easy to defer making decisions isn't it? You are probably subliminally waiting for some spur to action to occur. If, for example, your family members start to develop chills because of the draughty house, your old car finally gives up the ghost or your spouse expresses a desire to go abroad for some winter sun, that's when the spur to action arises. At that point, an effort is made to make the purchase. Until that moment, it remains dormant. All I did that day in John Lewis was to accidentally provide the sales assistant with a spur to action. Incidentally, he was so pleased that I had given him the excuse to put the savings plans into operation that he subsequently kindly introduced me to a rich seam of purchasers as he was evidently considered an influential and wise father figure by many young people in his area of London.

"Business is what,
when you don't have any,
you go out of."

(Unknown)

— CHAPTER THREE —

A Very Dodgy Start

A dark, damp and dreary evening turned into a terrifying descent - two hours later, a happy conclusion - but only from a business point-of-view.

Some years ago, an Accountant of my acquaintance asked me to make contact with some clients of his who were planning on emigrating to New Zealand. Apparently, the husband and wife needed some advice on how to invest a substantial amount of money here in the UK whilst they were planning on living in New Zealand.

I telephoned the couple and was told by the husband to meet him in a car park in Shoreham-by-Sea that Tuesday evening. The meeting took place in October on a cold and foggy evening. I duly arrived at the appointed time, got out of the car and stood in as conspicuous a spot among the puddles as I could find to await the arrival of my prospective client. I stood shivering in the cold night air accompanied by the paraphernalia of my work : my trusty briefcase, a rather heavy laptop computer and a compact printer.

The car park, I should explain, overlooked the sea and was very poorly lit. After a few minutes, an indistinct figure walked towards me through the gloom and asked me if I was John Shorter. Following a brief hello and the customary handshake, he strode out at speed towards the edge of the carpark leaving me to struggle with my equipment on my own. I had no alternative but to follow him avoiding the many puddles as best as I could. I was uncertain as to where my new prospective client was heading. He was striding out purposefully towards the edge of the car-park and the sea beyond as far as I could make out. When we ran out of ground, all became clear. It appeared that he and his wife were planning on sailing to New Zealand in an old sailing boat. I peered into the gloom down over the edge of the car park and found myself looking down onto the top of the boat's mast with the deck some thirty foot below! I have never felt comfortable at heights. In fact, I get giddy when I've got thick socks on. Frankly, there in the inky blackness of a moonless October with a 30 foot descent before me, I was terrified. My friend knelt down and then, advancing backwards without a word, went over the edge of the car park and disappeared down some ancient iron steps which were let into the ancient slimy green wall. The effortless speed with which he carried out this manoeuvre showed that he was totally familiar with this exercise. I had no alternative but to follow.

So, with my heavy briefcase in one hand, the printer in the other and the laptop computer strapped to my back, I commenced the long perilous downward journey to the deck. I was so relieved to step onto the relative safely of the steel deck and somewhat surprised that my would-be client had neither offered a helping hand nor even said a word to me since he had started his downward journey from the car-park.

The next hour or two passed without incident and I felt much more at ease presenting my proposals to him and his wife over a cup of coffee. The reverse journey in the pitch black evening back to my car was just as frightening as the earlier descent. Again, I was given no help. The shoe-full of filthy water I collected as I stepped right into a rain-filled pothole near my car put the cap on what had been a less than enjoyable evening.

My nautical friends remained clients for quite a few years once they arrived in New Zealand but I will not forget the dangers and discomfort I endured that cold October evening.

"I commenced the long perilous downward journey to the deck".

Sometimes, even the most miserable experience can turn out well in the end. That particular winter's evening didn't start well for me. I had driven for over an hour in foggy conditions and pouring rain before I arrived at a God-forsaken meeting point where a rather saturnine figure met me in the gloom. Thence followed the terrifying experience of a descent down a wet, slippery and rusty ladder to the boat's deck below. I had every reason to believe that the experience would continue in this negative vein until it was time to drive all the way home again.

Something told me, however, that the miserable feelings I was experiencing were only happening to me - not my prospective client or his wife who was in the galley making a hot cup of coffee for the three of us. In fact, the evening passed rather pleasantly with me doing what I enjoyed most, explaining and educating. My hosts seemed to me to be very attentive and interested in what I had to say and all was conducted within the warm and cosy interior of a ship-shape little craft. At the end of a couple of hours of fact-gathering, it was agreed that at the next meeting which would be on dry land, forms would be filled in and investments initiated. Thus it occurred a couple of weeks later.

Had I allowed the unpromising beginnings to dominate the proceedings, there might well have been a very different conclusion. As it was, these clients remained loyal to my firm for many years. Putting other people's desires and requirements ahead of one's own discomfort usually pays dividends and provides benefits to both parties.

As was my habit, on the hour or so drive back home that night, I conducted the autopsy to see if any lessons could be learned. The glaring fact which hit me was that it is so important to look at things from the other guy's point-of-view. I was not in the best of moods when I met my client but what does that matter? How is that relevant? What is crucial is to put his position centre stage - not mine.

Why didn't he help me with the cumbersome paraphernalia I had brought with me? He, having carried the shopping up and down those perilous iron steps hundreds of times didn't give me another thought. Why should he?

— CHAPTER FOUR —

Saturday in Islington

A difficult journey to a reluctant prospect - my summary dismissal - Limping home to live another day.

Many years ago when my long-suffering wife, Vivienne, was a mere girlfriend, I had an appointment to meet a young girl called Pearl in Islington to discuss savings plans. Pearl originally came from St Lucia and she lived with numerous relatives in a square of rather neglected houses in Islington. As Pearl was unable to grant me an audience during the working week, she had suggested that it would be convenient for her if we meet on a Saturday morning at 9.30 a.m. at her home. I persuaded Vivienne to accompany me on the two-hour car journey from the wilds of East Sussex (I doubt whether I'd be able to persuade her to undertake such a trip these days!). I was very proud of my shiny second hand Ford Capri which was to convey us there.

We set off in torrential rain very early that Saturday morning so we would be sure to arrive in good time. So it was that we finally arrived outside Pearl's parents' rather seedy-looking home at just before 9.30 a.m. Vivienne agreed to sit patiently in the car while I conducted business within the house. As with many houses in that square, the front door was at the top of about six steps and I applied myself to the rusty knocker with some enthusiasm. I noticed as I did so that the second hand on my wristwatch swept up to the top of the dial. I could also hear a distant church bell tolling the half-hour. Pearl would surely be highly impressed with my timekeeping if nothing else! After a few minutes, I knocked again. Nothing stirred within. For some reason, I looked down to the lower ground beneath the six steps where there was a small very dirt-encrusted window. At first, I saw only the grime and darkness beyond but, as my eyes became accustomed to the gloom, I saw the whites of two nervous eyes looking up at me. Unmistakably, these belonged to Pearl. I couldn't understand why she didn't just run up the stairs to let me in. After all, we had an appointment, didn't we?

While I was still pondering on Pearl's unexpected behaviour which was bordering on downright rudeness, a mature female voice boomed at me at waist level through the letterbox in a thick Caribbean accent, "What do you want?". I must admit that I was not a little taken aback by this somewhat aggressive tone but nonetheless kept my cool and informed my enquirer that my name was John Shorter from Abbey Life and that I had an appointment with Pearl. This aggravated the lady and she said that if I didn't leave straightaway, she would call the police. She said that she was Pearl's mother and that neither she nor her daughter had any need for life assurance thank you.

Despite my disappointment at not even having been given a chance to exercise my skills of persuasion that cold and blustery Saturday morning, I considered the appropriate course of action was to retreat. It was therefore with heavy hearts that we drove back to Ticehurst to enjoy what was left of the weekend. I forced myself to remember the words of the Frank Crumit song, "There's No One With Endurance Like The Man Who Sells Insurance". (Go on, Google it!).

For the best part of the journey home, I found myself justifying to Vivienne why anyone would wish to earn a living by willingly subjecting himself to the expense, frustration and indignity of such rejection as we had just witnessed.

Little did either of us realise at the time that this unfortunate experience was one of many building-blocks of a career which was to span 40 years.

"I saw the whites of two nervous eyes looking up at me".

This unfortunate experience took place during one of the very early years of my career. As the years progressed, of course, I developed a natural resistance to allowing prospective clients to hold the whip hand in this type of situation. In those early days, however, every meeting represents an important opportunity to create another loyal client.

By listening and learning how other, more experienced, practitioners operated I was enabled to choose dates and times to suit my calendar rather than the client's. I learned that one loses no Brownie Points by saying that one already has an appointment at that time (even if it is a little white lie). The more accessible the sales person/adviser proclaims himself to be, the greater the chance that he/she is giving the impression that it is the client who holds the power to control the appointment. The same could be said of almost any other trade or profession. I always remember the story of the commercial traveller who puts up in a Welsh B&B the night before his early morning appointment with a prospective customer. He found himself with a little time on his hands that wet evening and decided to spend some time going to the pictures in a neighbouring town. He 'phoned up to find out the time of the last complete performance and the projectionist said, "It's up to you bach, What time can you get here?".

"It isn't what I do,
but how I do it.
It isn't what I say,
but how I say it,
and how I look when I do it
and say it."

(Mae West)

— CHAPTER FIVE —

An Unfortunate Misunderstanding

An encounter in my office with a man of God - His deaf, almost mute, wife - Being put in my place.

One day I was sitting minding my own business (literally) in my Dyke House offices when I received an unexpected visit from a member of the clergy. The elderly and somewhat infirm vicar had read an article I had had published in the local newspaper and sought some financial advice. It appeared that he and his wife had inherited some capital and were at a loss as to how best to invest it. After a very pleasant half hour chat with the gentleman, it was clear to us both that we would get along well. He proposed to me that I should meet his dear wife and that we should all run through some investment ideas together. For that reason, he suggested that we should meet the following afternoon at their house.

He met me at the door and confidentially mentioned to me that his wife was profoundly deaf and might have some difficulty in hearing or understanding me unless I made an effort to enunciate very loudly and clearly. I agreed to bear that in mind and he took me into their sitting room where his rather imperious wife, Sybil, was sitting in a large antique armchair. The dear lady looked at me with rheumy eyes and gave me a pleasant smile. I approached her and extended my hand in greeting. She shook it weakly with her cool bony fingers. I was then motioned towards an overstuffed settee upon which I parked myself. A desperately awkward three-way conversation then took place. In a very loud voice, the vicar would say something to me. Out of respect for his wife, Sybil, we would then glance together at her for a comment. It failed to materialise. Then I would have a go. Loud voice, glance to Sybil. Nothing. This ritual was repeated several times. As the points being raised by the vicar and me were all trivial niceties anyway, we soon reached the point when there seemed little reason to continue the process and I was frankly relieved when the vicar suggested that a nice cup of tea was called for. It was obvious to us both that poor Sybil had not yet heard a single word.

While the vicar was clinking the crockery in the kitchen, I looked around the large sitting room and saw that it was full of beautiful antique furniture and bric-a-brac much of which was either Victorian or Georgian. It was clear that the vicar and his wife had either both come from wealthy families or that they were avid collectors of quality furniture.

After a minute or two, I felt a little awkward that I was examining my surroundings much as a Brighton antique dealer might in the same situation. It was necessary for me to say something to Sybil to break the silence. She was obviously determined to remain mute and so it was left to me to initiate some conversation. Unusually, I found it quite difficult to know exactly what to say. I looked around the room for inspiration and my eyes alighted on a very pretty yew corner cupboard which I felt was probably 18th century. Relieved to have found something to talk about, I said, rather loudly as I had been instructed, "What a beautiful corner cupboard. It's yew isn't it?". At first, she failed to hear what I was saying and asked me to speak up a little. Once more, a little more loudly this time, "Your lovely corner cupboard – it's yew isn't it?". She then replied, a little indignantly I thought, "Oh good heavens no, we've had it for years".

This little tale serves to illustrate that a successful outcome does not necessarily require all the parties involved to understand (or even to hear) the solutions being recommended! This delightful couple became and remained investors for many years until they both passed away.

I would suggest that the reason that they bought the investment proposition which I recommended was that the vicar trusted me perhaps because he had read my article in the local newspaper which he trusted. His wife Sybil trusted her husband and so, when he demonstrated to her that he trusted me, she trusted him. So long as that wonderful trust is never abused, taken advantage of or misused by the person being trusted, it can create the most satisfactory outcomes for all the parties involved.

"*It was necessary for me to say something to Sybil to break the silence*".

— CHAPTER SIX —

In the Nick of Time

*A real concern about Inheritance Tax
- Waning enthusiasm for the solution
- Delay of a year and then panic
- All's well in the end.*

I honestly cannot recall how it came about that I found myself one day talking to a wonderful old lady in her 80s in an elegant apartment near Brighton. Mrs Fortescue was concerned about Inheritance Tax and the dramatic effect it would have upon her adult childrens' legacy some day when she inevitably passed on.

She was one of those ladies who still had an inner beauty which was difficult to miss. I remember thinking that she had probably been very attractive as a young girl. Indeed, an early photograph of her in a silver frame on a sideboard proved the fact. Her husband had died a number of years earlier and she had inherited a share portfolio of considerable size. As is so often the case, neither she nor anyone else actively managed it for her. These shares, together with other assets, including the apartment itself, meant that IHT was a real threat. She had two sons and daughter. That first fact-finding meeting must have lasted a couple of hours and it was, as I recall, a pleasurable experience for both of us. Back in the office, I assimilated all the facts and wrote a comprehensive report for which no charge was made. A couple of weeks later, I telephoned Mrs Fortescue and made an appointment to see her again. I suggested that she might like to arrange for her adult children to be present too. During our subsequent meeting, which was attended by one of the sons (an Accountant by profession), Mrs Fortescue's daughter and a very experienced technical expert from the Insurance Company whose product I was recommending, I got the feeling that there was some resistance to the ideas I was proposing. I could not quite understand where the lack of enthusiasm was coming from and put it down to the very common reluctance to embrace any change to the status quo. The meeting, which again lasted a couple of hours, ended with the dreaded words, "Well, you've given us a lot to think about" ringing in my ears.

Several months went by and, after several telephone attempts on my part to re-kindle enthusiasm, my words seemed to fall on deaf ears. This, I thought was a 'china egg' which would never hatch! A few more months went by and I finally and reluctantly filed the papers away and forgot the whole experience.

I was amazed a year or so later one Wednesday evening to receive a 'phone call from the Accountant son to say that his mother was gravely ill in hospital and was not expected to survive for more than a few days. He asked me to put in hand the proposal which I had made almost a year earlier. This was totally out of the question as it would normally involve several weeks, if not months, to implement. He expressed disappointment and started to resign himself to the fact that a substantial amount of Inheritance Tax would be unavoidable. I initially agreed with him and resisted, with some difficulty, the temptation to say that this situation could have been easily averted if he had only agreed to proceed with my proposals twelve months or so earlier. In the back of my mind, however, I recall having read of socalled "death-bed schemes" which could legitimately avoid Inheritance Tax where clients had left things too late, as in this case, to do anything about it. I promised to look into the matter urgently. I did so the next morning on the Thursday and, following a number of frantic 'phone calls to people more familiar than me to this somewhat unusual form of financial planning, managed to piece a strategy together which might just work. That day, I met the interested parties at the hospital where Mrs Fortescue had been taken to spend her last days. I obtained all their signatures on papers which had all been prepared and produced in a matter of hours.

The death-bed scheme I had identified was offered by a specialist firm operating out of the Isle of Man and there was clearly no time to handle the matter by post in the normal way. I would have to go to the Isle of Man myself to ensure that the plan was implemented properly. This was a race against time as Mrs Fortescue was quite clearly very ill indeed.

I obtained the agreement of the family members to act on their behalf and set off for Gatwick on leaving the hospital. It was verbally agreed that any expenses I incurred would naturally be reimbursed to me.

I stayed in Gatwick overnight and caught a very early plane the following morning – a Friday. Then followed a very full day of checking the complicated documents, obtaining more signatures from local solicitors, banks etc. and I was assured by the expert manager in charge that everything was in order. The attention to detail which he brought to bear on the subject was very impressive. Although time was of the essence, he insisted upon checking and then checking again in an extremely pedantic way that all was in order. I was told that all the signatures, counter-signatures, dates and seals were all in place. Now the necessary approval would have to be sought from HM Revenue and Customs. This could take a considerable amount of time. I was told by the Manager that one missing signature or wrong date could be disastrous and would lead to the failure of the plan. No wonder he was Mr Fastidious!

I flew home on the Friday evening totally mentally and physically drained. I telephoned the Accountant son and discovered that his mother was still clinging to life – just.

"I flew home on the Friday evening totally mentally and physically drained".

Several nail-biting years elapsed before we received official confirmation that the plan had been approved by HMRC but approved it finally was. Nearly £400,000 of Inheritance Tax had been legitimately avoided all within the rules and completely legally. It was at about that time that the Government embarked upon the course of tightening up all the rules and I later discovered that the plan we had used was discontinued by the authorities but we had got our application in in good time.

It took some months and several reminders to recover my expenses from the Accountant son but it all ended well in the end.

By the way, Mrs Fortescue passed away on the Saturday morning, a matter of hours after I had got back from the Isle of Man. Experiences such as this reinforced in the mind that mine was a noble profession and one of which all good practitioners should be proud.

I believe it was once Lord Jenkins of Hillhead, a former Chancellor of the Exchequer, who said, "Inheritance Tax is a voluntary tax, paid by those who distrust their heirs more than they dislike the Inland Revenue!"

One of the things which caused me to enjoy my career so much was finding myself in the company of delightful individuals with whom I felt empathy. Mrs Fortescue was a good example. She was highly attractive to me on several levels. Not only was she vivacious, sophisticated and obviously very well-educated but she was also an excellent listener who had the old-fashioned manners to be quiet while I was talking. In turn, when I sensed that it was her turn to speak, I likewise paid her the courtesy of waiting until she had quite finished before I reacted to what she had said. It was in this spirit of polite verbal ping pong that we spent a couple of very pleasant hours together when we first met.

If the subject of our meeting had not been so complex, I have little doubt that we would have concluded business together very readily, such was the mutual respect and trust which we generated. As it was, however, three others joined us for the second meeting and all the dynamics inevitably changed. All progress frustratingly ground to a halt. I knew in my heart of hearts that what I had proposed during that meeting with all five of us present would satisfy the family's desire to reduce the burden of Inheritance Tax in a simple and totally legitimate way. However, the family members felt that the fullest consideration should be given to the proposal. That, in itself, is eminently sensible of course. The trouble was that the practical issues of the family members all getting together (their homes were separated by many hours of driving) proved to be too difficult and the decision to proceed withered on the vine. It wasn't until many months later, over a year in fact, that an unfortunate change in Mrs Fortescue's health concentrated the minds of the family on the substantial financial problem now facing them. The Accountant son called me and, following some deft footwork, a new solution was put in place which saved the day. On thinking afterwards of the way matters eventually played out, it occurred to me that, if I had shown any kind of annoyance that I had, in effect, wasted my time when the first recommendation was ignored, the Accountant would surely never have made that call to me a year a year later.

The importance of always maintaining a good relationship with people (whether they become clients or not) cannot be over-emphasised. Any hint of lack of patience on my part would probably have resulted in the family's fortune being seriously damaged. The only winner would have been HMRC.

— CHAPTER SEVEN —

Piss-catorial Pursuits

A very long car journey followed by several hours of heavy drinking - the elusive WC - much-needed relief.

I would like to recount an adventure which I had in 1973 with someone with whom I worked alongside in financial services. We both shared an interest in trout-fishing and had made a trip together to Scotland in his new Jaguar. After a very long car journey, we finally arrived at his cousin's house. Have you ever woken up in the dead of night as a guest in an unfamiliar house and been unable, try as you may, to find the door or light-switch which would lead you to the comfort of a much-needed smallest room? This happened to this colleague of mine during the trout-fishing weekend near Glasgow which we shared together. We had been out on the tiles with some hard-drinking local lads until some unearthly hour. My companion, rather the worse for wear I am afraid, retired gratefully to his bed immediately upon arrival at our host's home. It is my custom always to read for a half-hour or so before attempting to sleep and this, I did, despite the lateness of the hour.

I had hardly put my copy of "Advanced Salesmanship" down, it seemed, when I was immersed in deep slumber. Imagine my surprise when I was violently awakened in the inky blackness by the form of my colleague as it fell upon me in a crumpled heap. Amid much cursing and incoherent mumblings (with a complete lack of apology I might add), it arose and started off on a circular tour of the bedroom which we were sharing. I recalled reading somewhere that it can be dangerous to attempt to awake a sleepwalker, for that it what I thought he was at the time, so I held my peace.

In this bedroom, there were two walk-in cupboards, one wardrobe and a bona fide exit. The total time spent by my friend on the first of the two cupboard doors was, I estimated about three minutes. Surely a record for persistency! Finally, he managed to unlock and disappear through the third door. No sooner had this happened than he emerged again. His somewhat befuddled brain advised him that little relief was to be gained in there.

I sat and listened no longer. I could sense that he was coming across the room in my direction once more and was in no mood to weather a further assault from someone in his parlous state. With thoughts in mind of our genial hosts asleep in the neighbouring bedroom, I asked my partner, in whispered tones, exactly what the matter might be. "I want to go to the toilet" he replied in a desperate voice designed to elicit sympathy on my part. Being in this unfortunate, not to say dangerous predicament, I felt obliged to help all I could and therefore resolved without delay to locate the exit door to the landing and thus to that oasis he so earnestly sought. In no time I found another door for him which I genuinely believed was the exit. With a gentle push, I propelled him through into the uncharted darkness beyond. It was in graphic language that my frustrated friend advised me of my error. It was, unfortunately, the wardrobe – again.

I think it was at this point in the proceedings that the humour of the situation suddenly struck us both. We dissolved into uncontrollable mirth there in the darkness of that room with no exit. If any action is designed to precipitate disaster for anyone in his already uncomfortable condition it is that of hysterical laughter. With a brave summonsing of willpower that neither of us knew we possessed, we launched a renewed attack upon any possible exits there might be with a sense of urgency. It was during this second effort of mine that my desperate colleague was heard to mutter that the window was the only feasible answer.

I actually imagined these unseemly utterings to be from his drink-fuelled brain and diligently continued my search for the elusive door without too much heed. It was only when I clearly heard splashing upon the concrete patio twenty feet below that I realised just what a terrible state my pal must have been in. Just then, I found the door itself and with great control he accordingly transferred his attention mid-stream from the window to the appropriate facility which had been provided for the purpose on the landing.

Finding our bedroom once more presented him with a further problem but, following a brief visit to our host's bedroom, he re-joined me to spend the remainder of the night without incident.

NB My trout-fishing friend was John Handelaar and I am John Shorter.

"My desperate colleague was heard to mutter that the window was the only feasible answer".

The only lesson which I drew from this experience is that it is seldom a good idea to down eight pints of heavy without knowing where the toilet is!

— CHAPTER EIGHT —

Selling and Mis-selling

*Becoming more discerning with my choice of client
- Offering the right solution for the client
- An Accountant destroys my client's confidence in me
- Dire financial consequences for the family.*

In the early days of my selling career, I was far less discerning than I later became – as far as prospective clients were concerned. I would have been quite happy to sign up anything that could walk, crawl or fly.

At one point, I found myself working within a seam of people in the construction industry. After a while, I noticed that a large number of policies I had sold to bricklayers, for example, had begun to lapse early. This resulted in a reversal of my commission which was clearly very unsatisfactory from my point-of-view. A similar pattern was emerging with plasterers, plumbers etc. so I made a decision to aim "up-market" and only deal with business-owners and directors of construction companies in the future. So it was that I found myself one evening talking to the owner of a very successful local scaffolding company. We shall call him Kevin. I remember that I was in the room he had allocated as an office in his home. There were papers and files piled high in this room and everything seemed hopelessly chaotic. However, we had a reasonable conversation and he readily grasped the points I was putting forward. "Would your wife be able to cope financially if you were unexpectedly taken from us?", "Would your wife and three boys (all under 10) be able to carry on in the business as usual if some fatal accident or illness were to strike you down?" and so on. Like so many people of his age (mid-forties) Kevin's only experience with Life Assurance up to that point had been through "The Man from the Pru" or one of the other Industrial Offices. The total cover on his life amounted to £2,000 or some such paltry figure. This on a man who was taking an annual salary of £25,000 from his successful company even in 1980 or thereabouts. I recommended that at least £100,000 of life cover should be applied for. He readily agreed and we made an arrangement to meet a week later to complete the Application Form once I had set out the proposal in writing for him. That first meeting lasted two hours and I came away with a comprehensively-completed Fact Find.

The following week, we had our second meeting as planned. I gave him two options. I asked Kevin whether he wanted permanent cover which would last all his life or whether he wanted to take out the policy for a specific number of years. I pointed out that the permanent policy, whilst obviously more expensive, would build up a surrender value as the years progressed so that, if the policy was deemed unnecessary at some point on the future, there would be an opportunity to encash it thus reducing or even eliminating the premiums already paid. The temporary policy, on the other hand, would never acquire a cash value and the only way to benefit from it would be to make sure that he died within the chosen term!

As he felt that he could easily afford the permanent policy, he applied for that one. I should mention at this point that Kevin was very fit. One could see the muscles rippling beneath his tee-shirt and his skin was the colour of mahogany – the mark of a man who spent all his time working outside. I had little doubt that he would pass the Medical Examination with flying colours. Two weeks later, I had the pleasure to ring Kevin to let him know the good news. He had been accepted by the Insurance Company on standard terms.

I thought that Kevin would be pleased to hear this news but his reaction surprised me. He said he wanted to run it by his Accountant first. I said that I would be only too pleased to meet him and to run through the discussions which Kevin and I had had together. Kevin insisted, however, that it would not be necessary but that he would show the paperwork to the Accountant himself. It was suggested that I should call Kevin back in two weeks to give him the opportunity to have his meeting in the meantime.

I had had prior experience of Accountants and had seen before how they can derail the plans laid by the most skilful and experienced financial advisers. I was therefore quite nervous of the outcome although I knew that Kevin had come to the appropriate decision having taken all the facts into account. I felt, however, that I was no longer in control of the situation.

"Who should serve me with my cuppa but Pam".

Three weeks later, to the day, I telephoned Kevin who told me that the Accountant's view was that the policy I had put forward was unnecessarily expensive! I was told that the Accountant had promised to find something more suited to my client's needs! I was upset that my professionalism had been questioned. It did little to improve the relationship between Kevin and me – in fact, it had driven a wedge between us. I sensed a definite frostiness which had certainly not existed before. Kevin promised to get back to me if the Accountant found nothing better than I had proposed. Some hope, I thought. How could I hope to compete for Kevin's loyalty when the Accountant and he had known each other for ten years? I'm not prone to giving up easily but it seemed to me to be a hopeless case. It would be an easy job for the Accountant to rubbish my recommendation and to replace it with his own. In those days, it was very common for Insurance Companies to hand out Commission Agreements to almost anyone who wanted one. They wanted the business and often showed scant regard as to where it came from. A week or so later, not having heard from Kevin, I called him only to be told that the Accountant had recommended the **temporary** solution as it was much cheaper. Of course it was cheaper but we had discussed all that hadn't we? It was at that point that I reluctantly gave up the unequal struggle. Quite what the Accountant had said to Kevin about my recommendation I will never know but the end result was to rubbish my advice and to destroy our budding relationship. Kevin's wife, Pam had had very little to do with the decision-making. In fact, I'd only met her twice – on each occasion when she had kindly brought me a cup of tea. Kevin was obviously the decision-maker and what he said went. It was with great surprise that I received a telephone call from Pam some weeks later at home. Fighting back the tears, she told me that Kevin had suffered a massive heart attack and had died the day before. She understood that Kevin and I had taken steps to put a £100,000 life assurance policy in place and she was understandably looking for confirmation that it would now pay out. Without wishing to scare her in any way, I explained that the Company's Accountant was also involved and that she should call him too. It occurred to me that, whether it was my permanent policy or his preferred temporary solution which paid out, it would not matter as long as a current policy provided Pam with the much needed cash at this crucial time. The facts eventually emerged. It appears that the Accountant, in his haste to replace the applied-for policy with one of his own choosing had committed the cardinal sin. He had thrown away the "dirty water" before replacing it with "clean". He told Kevin to write to the Insurance Company to cancel the Application which I was arranging before he replaced it with his temporary solution. In fact, I discovered, he had not even helped Kevin to fill in an Application Form by the time Kevin had so sadly and unexpectedly died. Poor Pam, therefore, received nothing from anybody (except the £2,000 from the Prudential).

I was so angry on Pam's behalf that, through the selfish action of the Accountant, she had missed out on £100,000 which should have been rightly paid to her that I telephoned the Accountant and gave him a piece of my mind. I told him that he was a disgrace to his profession and that his appalling behaviour should be exposed. He remained totally without remorse and put down the receiver while I was still mid-sentence.

Some years later, I popped into a run-down café for a spot of breakfast. Who should serve me with my cuppa but Pam? How her fortunes had changed. From director's wife to waitress. It could have been so different if the magic of life assurance had been given a chance to work properly.

I explained to Pam exactly what had happened but she shrugged her shoulders and said, "Oh well, that's life". The anger welled up within me when I remembered the telephone conversation I had had with Accountant but I felt that if Pam, the actual victim of the situation, was prepared to let it go, then I should as well.

This was a case where I felt I had acted diligently and professionally throughout on behalf of my client and yet my efforts had been thwarted by a commission-hungry Accountant to the detriment of Kevin's widow and young family. I well recall how angry I was when I realised what had happened. I still feel that anger even though the event occurred more than forty years ago!

With the benefit of hindsight and with more life experience I might have handled things differently. At the point when Kevin told me that he wanted to show the paperwork to his Accountant, I should have had the courage to refuse to allow that to happen. It would have been better if I had politely offered to run through the alternative schemes with the Accountant - either with or without Kevin being present (the former being favourite). By effectively allowing the client to do my job for me, I actually lost all control of the situation.

As events panned out, through the intervention of the Accountant, Pam and her family missed out big time, the Accountant gained nothing because he neglected to arrange the replacement temporary policy and I too had wasted all my time and effort. I resolved that I would always retain control of similar situations in the future.

"There are two things to
aim at in life:
first, to get what you want;
and after that, to enjoy it.
Only the wisest of mankind
achieve the second."

(Logan Pearsall Smith)

— CHAPTER NINE —

Poor Prospects

*Poor quality prospect - A reluctant welcome
- The mysterious canine
- Hopelessness recognised by both parties.*

A friend of mine, Christine, tells the story of a business meeting she had early on in her career. It appears that she had an appointment to discuss financial planning matters with a man who lived alone on a particularly run-down Council estate. She arrived in good time for the liaison but it was with a heavy heart that she realised the house where the meeting was to take place was the most neglected one in the street. The area of ground in front of the house, which could hardly be graced with the title of a garden, was chest-high with overgrown shrubs, plants and weeds which threatened to obscure the front gate altogether. However, Christine managed with some difficulty to open the gate which was only held in place by a solitary hinge. As she struggled through with her briefcase, she was startled by a low shadowy shape which brushed her leg as it sped down the pathway between the tall weeds. Arriving at the faded and dirty front door, she tried the knocker but found it badly rusted and immovable. A sharp rat-a-tat-tat with her pen did the trick and brought the occupant shuffling to the door from the dark interior. As soon as the door was opened by an adequate amount, the shadowy shape which had preceded her down the jungle path, squeezed through and ran into the hall and then into a room beyond. It was, as far as she could make out, some sort of dull-looking mongrel dog.

The man stood in the doorway and seemed to be confused as to whom his smartly-dressed briefcase-bearer could be. Christine politely introduced herself and reminded the man, who had clearly forgotten, that an appointment had been made to discuss his financial affairs. The man, who looked as though he had just awoken from deep sleep, mumbled something incoherent and padded off to the room beyond. Christine followed and found herself in a dimly-lit square rather stale-smelling room with two badly-stained armchairs, an oak table and an assortment of books, old magazines and newspapers strewn about. It was a room which offered little comfort except that there was a coal fire in front of which the mongrel was stretched out on the moth-eaten carpet. An awkward moment ensued during which the man (sporting a grubby string vest no less) said nothing. Christine, keen to allow the silence no time to develop further, opened the batting by reminding her host that the appointment had been made for her by an agency she was using at the time, specifically to discuss savings plans, life assurance, pensions and other products which may be relevant from her armoury. Being very quick on the uptake, Christine deduced at the front gate stage that the chances of lucrative business being concluded, were distinctly slim, but nevertheless felt it was incumbent on her to "go through the motions". She therefore embarked upon her usual opening spiel with as much enthusiasm as she could muster.

Fifteen minutes into her introduction, however, she began to think that her skills should be directed to a much more appreciative audience elsewhere. The man had offered not one word throughout Christine's little speech and it was very obvious that he was finding the meeting very boring if not

"The mongrel dog let forth a yellow stream".

totally irrelevant to him. Christine was considering in her sub-conscious mind how she may bring this unfortunate meeting to an end when something very odd occurred. The mongrel dog who had made only the occasional grunt throughout Christine's address, got up, stretched and very deliberately cocked its leg against one of the table's legs and let forth a yellow stream which proceeded to dribble down on to the carpet. Its business done, it returned to the warmth of the fireside to resume its sleep. The man said nothing but continued to stare into space as before. This example of what an untrained dog will do when left to its own devices unchecked explained the stale pungent smell which pervaded the house.

After what she had just witnessed, Christine couldn't wait to call it a day and to quit the premises without any further delay. She felt the time had come for the man to offer some sort of response. She therefore asked him if anything she had said so far had struck a chord with him. It was evident that the man was equally keen to bring things to an early closure when he said that Christine had raised a lot of interesting points which he said he would have to think about. Even though Christine was at an early stage of her career at the time, she recognised that the man's response was an excuse to abort the meeting. So he wanted out as much as she did! Christine wasted no time and gathered up her papers into her briefcase. She was grateful to hear the time-honoured words "I'll let you know if I'm interested" – another way of saying "Go away and don't come back!". Christine gratefully exited the front door and, having bid the man adieu (A euphemism for "Let me out of this hell-hole"), beat her way to the gate. She had only taken a few steps towards her car when she heard the man shout out, "Hey, don't forget your dog!".

This was a disastrous meeting from the giddy-up. Christine herself would never have specifically chosen a prospective client with such low promise. It was the Agency she was using at the time who arranged the appointment. On the supposition that every experience should be helpful in building one's career, this unfortunate encounter offered at best the opportunity to go back to the Agency to clearly re-define the target clientele.

Many years ago, I too used the services of a lady who lived next door to make appointments for me with people whose names appeared on a list which I had bought. Our relationship failed, however, when I travelled for an hour or more to see a prospective client who was clearly under the misguided impression that I was applying for the position of a jobbing gardener!

The problem, of course, is that one has very little control over what your chosen Agent actually says when 'phoning on your behalf.

"The futility of riches is stated very plainly in two places, the Bible and the income tax form."

(Anon)

— CHAPTER TEN —

The Right Choice

*Brilliantly clever prospect - A desire to become mortgage-free as soon as possible
- A secure future seemed assured
- Safeguarding against the unlikely event
- My persuasive tactics proved to be unexpectedly valuable.*

About twenty years ago, a local Accountant with whom I had a very agreeable business relationship, contacted me and explained that one of his very successful clients was in need of some serious financial planning. It appeared that his client, Phil, was a telecommunications engineer whose overseas contract had recently come to an end. He had been solely responsible for the installation of an entire telephonic network in an Eastern European country. The mammoth job, having been completed, he had returned to the UK to be reunited with his wife, Helen, after his prolonged absence abroad. More lucrative UK contracts were in the offing and the future looked pretty rosy for them. I met them both one evening in a beautifully appointed modern house in Brighton Marina. They had purchased it a few months earlier with the help of a substantial mortgage. Surrounding houses were increasing in value each year and it promised to be an excellent investment for them. During that first meeting, Phil made it clear to me that his main concern was that he had never put any serious savings plans in place, either for the medium-term or for his eventual retirement. He and Helen were in their mid-forties. Also, the £230,000 mortgage was a millstone around their necks which he wanted to be rid of as soon as possible. His ambition was to be totally mortgage-free within five years. His annual income during the last few years had been considerable (about £200,000) and it had exceeded their outgoings by a factor of 6. Phil had calculated that he could easily afford to set aside £3,000 per month to provide for their future and was looking to me to recommend a range of financial products and Insurance Companies.

I asked Phil and Helen if their mortgage was "self-cancelling". They said they weren't quite sure what I meant by that. I explained that it was possible to ensure that, in the event of a death or serious illness occurring during the term of the mortgage, it would be immediately cancelled out thus making them debtfree at that point. Phil said that this was an attractive proposition and wanted to know the cost involved. I promised to get some figures together and to include them within the report of recommendation which I would provide at our next meeting.

A week or so later, we met in their house for a second time during which I presented my report. I recommended a range of tax-efficient savings arrangements to provide the means of paying back the mortgage early as he had wanted. Included within the £3,000 monthly outlay, I explained, would be a figure to make the mortgage "self-cancelling" as I had explained. Phil seemed very happy with my suggestions but questioned whether it was good value to divert any money into the "self-cancelling" part. After all, he said, he had always enjoyed good health and couldn't even recall when he had last visited the doctor. In short, he was prepared to go ahead with all my recommendations except that he wanted the entire £3,000 to be allocated to investment to provide for the fastest possible payback of the mortgage. The insurance premium to cater for an untimely death or critical illness was, in his view, simply a waste of money.

Recognising the danger that our very pleasant new friendship could be put under strain if I applied any kind of pressure, I nonetheless insisted that it would be eminently sensible to withhold about 10% of the monthly amount available to cater for the unthinkable events of death or critical illness. After all, I said, how on earth would Helen manage to meet the mortgage repayments each month if Phil was struck down with a serious illness or even death? In the end, rather reluctantly I thought, Phil gave in and agreed with my logic. We completed the paperwork for all the various plans I had recommended. Several weeks later, I delivered all the policy documents and we finally ran through the details together.

Two years later, I received the bad news that Phil had been struck down with lung cancer and was to undergo an operation the next week. I immediately put a claim in hand for them and, within a matter of weeks, the Insurance Company paid out £230,000 under the Critical Illness Policy. From that moment, Phil and Helen were indeed mortgage-free. At least, that was something they would never have to worry about again..

"In the end, rather reluctantly I thought, Phil gave in and agreed with my logic".

Phil's requirement was simple. Firstly, he wanted to be mortgage-free. Secondly, he wanted to save up in a tax-efficient way for the medium-term (i.e. in 10 years' time) and thirdly, he wanted to create a substantial income in retirement (i.e. in 20 years' time or so). These were his "wants". I felt, however, that his "needs" had been overlooked.

The prospect of his suffering a serious illness, or even death, during his working life he considered so unlikely that neither event was worth insuring against. Such is the strong belief that it always happens to someone else. In the event, he sadly became that "someone else" himself. I sometimes muse on the position that Helen would have found herself in had Phil dug his heels in and refused to buy the protection element upon which I had insisted.

I'm still in touch with Helen and she is now a widow. Sadly, Phil passed away when he eventually lost his battle with cancer. The additional life cover which I had arranged for him ensured that Helen was able to live largely self-sufficient in a mortgage-free home. I always felt satisfied that the job had been done correctly.

"These days, the Government spends as much accidentally as it did on purpose years ago."

(Bob Monkhouse)

John being presented in 1980 with his Million Dollar Round Table Membership certificate.

Early days - hard at work.

Pen at the ready.

Ken Davy of SimplyBiz presenting John with the International Quality Award.

John and Vivienne with (left to right) the Architect, the Furniture Designer and the Property Developer (in front of Church Farm, their home for the first 15 years).

John attends James Caan's Entrepreneurs Business Academy.

A few days off to catch salmon in Russia!

Our sons, Giles, Jerome and Alexander.

A man needs wheels - right?

One Hyde Gardens, Eastbourne from which the business operated (1991-2012).

Eastbourne's Mayor presents John with a silver biscuit barrel to commemorate 25 years in business (2005).

A garden party (in 2010) for friends and clients to help celebrate 30 years of the business (in front of Alderden Old Manor, their home for the second 15 years).

NEWS IN BRIEF

Herald, Friday, August 12, 2005 11

Million Dollar Round Table

JOHN Shorter, managing director of local Independent financial advisers Shorter Byrne and Co, attended the 2005 annual meeting in New Orleans of the prestigious Million Dollar Round Table, the premier association for financial advisers. His MDRT membership places him among the world's elite life assurance and financial services professionals.

The club, founded in 1927, is an international independent association of about 29,000, of the world's financial services professionals who have demonstrated superior product knowledge, exceptional client service and unquestionable ethical conduct.

John at the Million Dollar Round Table, New Orleans in 2005.

John and Vivienne with colleagues at One Hyde Gardens.

— CHAPTER ELEVEN —

A Fool and His Money...

Once-in-a-lifetime good fortune
- Hungry friends and relatives cruelly
cause the cash pile to dwindle
- No plans put in place for the future.

I once had a call from an Accountant of my acquaintance. It appeared that he had been approached by someone who had been lucky enough to have had a substantial win on the Lottery. We shall call him Peter. I was given a name, a telephone number and an address and asked to make an appointment to see what advice I could give. In a brief telephone conversation, we agreed to meet at Peter's house a few days later.

The modest modern house was on a Council estate. Many of the surrounding houses had overgrown front gardens and the usual sprinkling of rusty shopping trolleys and neglected children's plastic slides and so on. The feature which made Peter's house special was the very latest swish and shiny Chelsea Tractor which adorned the concrete standing. This was the first clue that Peter had started to take full advantage of his new-found wealth. I rang the doorbell and was greeted by a harassed young mother who identified herself as Peter's wife, Barbara. She had a small baby in her arms and another toddler clinging to her leg. I was invited into a small untidy living-room which was littered with the trappings of small children. Baby-walkers, tricycles, plastic toys were everywhere. The feint smell of used nappies pervaded the air. I sat down in a worn and grubby armchair and was offered a cup of tea which I politely declined. Barbara explained to me that Peter would be joining us but that he had been detained at his sister's new house a short walk away. While we waited for Peter, Barbara was kept very busy with the urgent needs of the small children.

Finally, Peter showed up and seemed to me to be in a very agitated frame-of-mind. It was clear that, whatever he had discussed with his sister had upset him. Anyway, I conducted the interview as well as I could. The interruptions were many and the unwatched TV which continued to blare out throughout the proceedings made serious conversation quite challenging. I gathered that Peter had won over £900,000 a few weeks previously but that, so far, it had afforded him less pleasure than he had hoped. The very flashy people-carrier which I had seen in front of the house was his only purchase. He explained that he had taken the opportunity of repaying some personal family debts and had paid off his credit card debit balance.

It transpired that Peter was a dustman (I'm sorry, I mean a waste disposal operative) who unsurprisingly had little experience of the investment of six-figure sums!

I was therefore working with a blank sheet of paper. Throughout our conversation, I found it quite difficult to pin Peter down, as far as figures were concerned. When I asked him how much was in his bank account, for example, he became very evasive. I found myself mentally calculating as follows:

He started off with about £900,000. Assuming he had paid cash for the people-carrier, say £60,000, the family- and credit card debts totalled say £50,000, he should have about £790,000 left over. But, when I pressed Peter for a figure, it seemed to me that he was talking about £350,000. In time, all became clearer. It appeared that his sister had persuaded him to buy her a house outright for £250,000! She had also prevailed upon him to give her a further £100,000. Three "friends" who all begged him for financial help accounted for a further £90,000. This had left Peter with £350,000 with which to secure his family's financial future. I had a further three meetings with Peter, Barbara and the children during which I put forward various tax-efficient ideas.

Alas, poor Peter became so overwhelmed with the decisions he had to make that eventually, he refused to see me again. Nothing was ever finalised with me. My guess is that he had listened to "the bloke down the pub" who probably persuaded Peter to invest the balance in some hare-brained scheme or other.

I felt it was so sad that this wonderful windfall which could have been used to alter the course of Peter and Barbara's lives was instead either squandered or "lent" to others. Nothing, of course, was ever put in writing. The money had given very little pleasure which only goes to prove the old saying, "A fool and his money....".

"The very latest swish and shiny Chelsea tractor which adorned the concrete standing".

This was one of the saddest situations I encountered in a long career. Th windfall which descended on Peter and Barbara gave them so little comfort. should have changed their lives and accordingly, those of their children. Instead through gullibility and the selfish actions of family and "friends", it provided fo them nothing but anxiety and concern. With thoughtful planning, the future o the whole family could have been made more secure. My guess is that Peter wi spend the rest of his life reflecting on what could have been.

— CHAPTER TWELVE —

Poor Timekeeping

A really bad start - Relaxation of tension leads to a productive meeting - Client's bank did me a favour - All's well that ends well.

One day in 1997(?), I received a telephone call from a gentleman who said he wanted to see me about a matter which was of the gravest importance to him. It was agreed that he would come to my office at 2.30 p.m. the following Tuesday afternoon. As I had no other meetings booked for that particular day, I envisaged a full morning dealing with paperwork, having a sandwich at my desk instead of going out for lunch and then being ready to see my new prospective client during the afternoon. The day looked well mapped-out ahead of me.

However, things seldom turn out as expected do they? At just after 1.00 p.m., a Representative from an Insurance Company showed up unannounced and said he had just attended a training session where he had learned about a brand new investment product which his Company intended to launch that very week. He apologised for the unexpected visit but justified it by saying that he wanted me to be the first adviser locally to learn about the new product. I should add that the quality and value of the Representatives who called on me varied widely. It was not my usual habit to admit a Rep just because he found it convenient to show up. This was a little different, however. Peter was one of the very best of the bunch and nearly always added benefit whenever I saw him. He was also, in my view, highly professional and knowledgeable in every way. Peter said that he would require about an hour of my time to explain the new product and suggested that we could have a light lunch over the road and have our business meeting there. I agreed but made the caveat that I absolutely must be back in the office for my 2.30 p.m. appointment. On his assurance that we had more than enough time, we set off together for the restaurant which was conveniently only two minutes' walk away.

As I had expected, the meeting was very productive and I was grateful to Peter for having brought the product to my attention so early thus enabling me to steal a march on my local competitors. Throughout the lunch, I had kept my eye on a clock which was located on the wall just above Peter's head. I started to get a bit twitchy when the clock told me it was 2.20 p.m. Just ten minutes to go! Just then, the door burst open and a group of people came in looking for a late lunch. The attention of the waitress was naturally directed to these new people and it took a bit longer than we expected to get the bill and to make our escape.

I had been told at the start of my career that accurate time-keeping was imperative in business. In fact, I had always prided myself on this very point and was disappointed that I was probably not going to make it to the office by the appointed time despite my best endeavours. I was right. I arrived ten minutes late in the end and found my prospective client, Vic and his daughter Lisa, in Reception looking none too thrilled to see me. He glared at me and was clearly upset at having been made to wait. "I was under the impression that we had agreed to meet at 2.30 p.m.", he said through gritted teeth. Of course, I apologised profusely but it was clear to me that the damage had already been done. With Vic's rebuke still ringing in my ears, I invited the two of them to accompany me to a private room upstairs where we could speak confidentially.

The meeting started off in a tense way but, as time went on, it started to become a little more relaxed. I thought that none of us would derive any benefit from the meeting if we allowed my unfortunate tardiness to dominate our thoughts. I therefore deliberately ignored the lateness of my arrival and instead concentrated upon the problem which Vic described to me. It appeared that his High Street bank who were "looking after" his investments had been treating him in a highly cavalier way. Firstly, he found it difficult to speak to the same person twice as they had usually been moved to another branch by the time he wanted to make contact. Secondly, he found it irksome and very tiresome in the extreme to have to go through the whole story all over again with the replacement employee. Furthermore, he found that a considerable fee was being taken from his investments each year and yet no discernible service was ever being rendered. It was obvious that Vic had had enough. The final insult occurred when he decided he would withdraw his money from the bank and was told that a huge penalty would then be imposed. His remonstrations to the bank had fallen on deaf ears and he was now at the end of his tether. As his story unfolded, I became totally sympathetic as to why he had been so upset with me half an hour earlier over what he saw as my sloppy timekeeping showing him no respect.

Our meeting, however, finished a little more friendly than it had started. After a couple of hours, I had all the information I required and I promised to do everything in my power to prove that not all advisers are money-grabbing heartless individuals. During the following week or so, I prepared my case and approached Vic's bank with as much diplomacy and firmness as I could muster. The end result was that I obtained the bank's eventual agreement to release the funds back to Vic without penalty.

"I was under the impression that we had agreed to meet at 2.30 p.m. he said through gritted teeth".

Over the next twenty years, I continued to look after Vic's financial affairs and I am pleased to say that matters progressed rather well. Vic and his wife, Carole, became very substantial clients of mine. Indeed, not merely clients, but friends too. Vic and I have travelled many miles together to attend AGMs, seminars and other business meetings and thoroughly enjoy each other's company as do our wives. A mutual sense of respect and affection now exists which few people would ever have envisaged from those first unfortunate minutes of our acquaintance. It just goes to show that, as the man says, all you have to do to succeed in business, is to make promises and then keep them. Incidentally, I have never been late for Vic since.

We all have our personal foibles. Our pet hates. Things that irritate us about others. In my case, if someone who is trying to sell me something gets my name wrong, for example, it is for me the kiss of death. My subconscious mind tells me in milliseconds that this person couldn't even be bothered to spell or pronounce may name correctly, he is therefore showing me a complete lack of respect and therefore does not deserve my business. Irrational and illogical though this is, it is how I feel.

Our problem is that we have no way of knowing in advance what prejudices exist in the mind of newly-encountered individuals. In the case of Vic, as I later discovered, his bête noire was (and remains) people who promise one thing and deliver another. I had promised to have a meeting with him at 2.30 p.m. but kept him waiting until 2.40 p.m. During that short period of time - just 10 minutes - he grew to dislike me! That explained his distinctly cool behaviour towards me at the start of our meeting. Of course, he had every right to be upset. From his point-of-view, I had shown him a total lack of respect by being late.
The fact that the atmosphere within our meeting gradually thawed out was very fortunate for me but it might just as easily have gone the other way. As it was, Vic and I became good friends and he, his wife Carole and his daughter Lisa all became loyal and substantial clients.

"There are two kinds of people,
the givers and the takers.
The takers eat well.
The givers sleep well".

(Anon)

— CHAPTER THIRTEEN —

Mixed Blessings

*A ten-year reluctance to discuss financial planning
- the breakthrough - plans implemented
- good news followed by bad news followed by good news.*

One of my favourite restaurants in the late seventies was on The Pantiles in Tunbridge Wells. It specialised in Swiss fare and was therefore somewhat unusual. The Head Waiter was exceptionally good at his job and made customers feel very welcome and special. In those days he always looked so smart in his bow-tie and immaculate dinner jacket and trousers. Peter was in his early thirties then although his quiet confidence and the effortless ease with which he carried out his duties would have been equally suited to an older man. He had a wife, Tilly, and a baby daughter.

Over the years, during which I enjoyed lunch or dinner there, I often thought of raising the subject of financial planning with Peter but somehow the opportunity never seemed to present itself. I was probably a bit reluctant to raise the sensitive subject of pensions or life assurance because a negative reaction on his part could have spoilt a very comfortable customer/Head Waiter relationship. Peter was well aware that I was a financial adviser but refrained from raising the subject with me, quite likely for the same reason. Who knows? We continued in that way for ten years or so. One day, however, during one of my visits to the restaurant in the company of a client of mine, Peter approached me confidentially at the end of the meal and asked me if I could find the time to discuss pensions with him. At that time, he would have been in his mid-forties and no doubt acutely aware that his life was slipping by. During a meeting I had with Peter a week or so later, it appeared that the owner of the restaurant, a Swiss nobleman of some sort, had consistently broken his promise to Peter to fund, for his benefit, a pension arrangement. It had become increasingly obvious to Peter that, unless he took steps to provide himself with some financial security in his retirement, no one was likely to do it for him. So it was that we started our business relationship together. A modest pension plan was preferable, we both agreed, to no pension at all. Over the years that followed, Peter and his wife Tilly, took out a number of plans through my company. Some Life Assurance, Permanent Health Insurance, savings plans, a Critical Illness Policy etc - all became eventually added to his portfolio. Nothing very dramatic but all sensible although modest premium stuff. Every six months or so, we would have a review meeting to ensure that everything was still up-to-date. Eventually, the Swiss restaurant closed down and the owner returned to live in Switzerland.

Peter was therefore forced to seek employment elsewhere. He took the opportunity to make a fresh start in a completely new career. He became a sales representative for a chemicals company. I personally felt that his sunny and generous personality suited him well for this line of work. He was doing very well and successfully building up his clientele when ill health first hit him. I learned of his problem when I received an anxious 'phone call from his wife Tilly. I should mention that, throughout my dealings with Peter, Tilly had always found an excuse to absent herself from the room whenever Peter and I started to talk about money. She always said she didn't understand these matters and preferred to leave "all that kind of thing" to Peter. A surprisingly common reaction within many families. Anyway, Tilly's call that evening came from the hospital where Peter had been admitted that very afternoon. Her

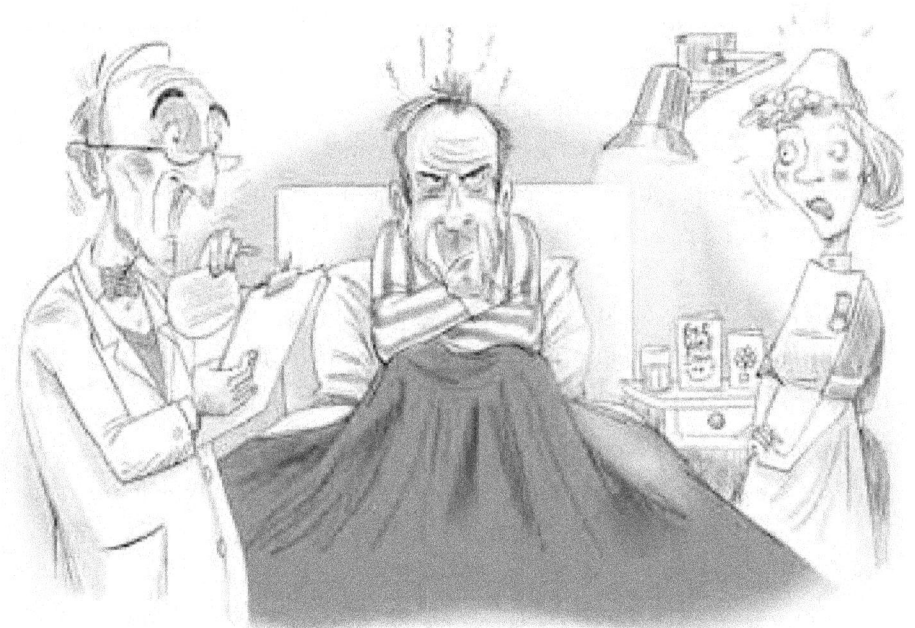

"This means I've still got the bloody mortgage", he said.

query was to ascertain whether the Critical Illness Policy I had set up on Peter a few months earlier was likely to pay out in view of the initial diagnosis of testicular cancer which Peter had been given that afternoon. I told Tilly that, subject to definite confirmation of the initial diagnosis, the policy would indeed pay out a substantial sum of money which Peter and I had targeted to repay the mortgage in full in one fell swoop. Peter had asked Tilly to find out the answer to his question and was probably holding his breath in his hospital bed pending the answer. She seemed very pleased to hear that the Insurance Company was likely to extinguish the debt and suddenly started to understand at that point what insurance was all about. I personally started to feel the satisfaction of a job well done. Of course, as I had pointed out, a successful claim depended totally upon a confirmed diagnosis.

Two days later, I received another call, this time from Peter. He wanted to hear directly from me, rather than through Tilly, just in case she had got it wrong! Again, I told him that, so long as the diagnosis of cancer was officially confirmed, he would no longer have to worry about repaying his mortgage. He said that this news had made him feel so much better and confident about his financial future, both short and long-term. We made an appointment to complete the Claim Form and he said he was expecting to to be able to provide the required proof very shortly as he had been told that the result of his biopsy was expected very soon.

I subsequently visited Peter in the hospital and helped him to complete the Claim Form and then sent it off for him. Later that week, I received another telephone call from Peter. This time, he seemed extremely upset and it took a few minutes for him to compose himself enough to reveal what he called his "bad news". It appeared that the doctors had just spoken to him and said that he did not have cancer after all. I was so pleased for Peter but asked him to explain to me how that could possibly be construed as bad news. "This means I've still got the bloody mortgage", he said. It took a few minutes for me to convince him that NOT having cancer after all was the best news he could possibly have received. This was one of the best examples of getting things out of perspective I had ever seen.

Unfortunately, a few years later, Peter sadly found that this episode was just the forerunner of a whole range of different illnesses which mercilessly descended upon him. One of these conditions beat him and he died at age 62.

I visited Tilly several times in the early stages of her widowhood but she seemed totally lost without her Peter. Sadly, she too passed away a couple of years later. The good news is that Tilly had no money worries during her final years thanks entirely to the additional Life Assurance policy I had arranged on Peter's life. When she died, Tilly's daughter received the proceeds of Tilly's life policy together with the residue of her late father's estate. That enabled her to start her married life from a very comfortable financial position. Personal financial planning had worked its magic again.

Why was I so reluctant for so long to raise the subject of financial planning with Peter? Answer: I was perhaps afraid that he wouldn't be interested and that it might spoil our future relationship. In actual fact, Peter was quite likely thinking something similar. His imagination may have been informing him that I might be upset if he raised the subject of pension planning with me. We were both wrong! When I did eventually arrange a modest pension plan for him, we both said what a pity but was that we hadn't taken the first steps ten years earlier. Making the initial approach to someone is always a bit nerve-racking for most of us. I have always found, however, that the event is seldom as scary as one's imagination might suggest.

"Too many people spend
money they earned
to buy things they don't want,
to impress people that
they don't like."

(Will Rogers)

— CHAPTER FOURTEEN —

Turnover is Vanity, Profit is Sanity

My involvement with a burgeoning computer software company - the flow of business over the years - the inevitable drying up of the well - realisation that profit is what matters.

An Accountant contact of mine once asked me to see two clients of his who were starting up a computer software company in Somerset. It involved a round trip for me of about eight hours by car. Having telephoned one of the directors, John, he told me that it would be appreciated if I could see them at 9.00 a.m. Under the circumstances, it seemed that an overnight stay nearby would be a sensible idea. I therefore booked myself into a modest hotel about two miles from where we would be meeting. After breakfast, I arrived in good spirits to meet my new prospective clients. The Accountant had told John and Alan (names changed) that a very substantial pension contribution was to be paid together with a sizeable monthly commitment thereafter. Accordingly, very little persuasion was called for on my part. Within an hour or so, John and Alan became my biggest clients. It was like falling off a log. This was one of those rarely-encountered occasions when an Accountant completely understood the tax advantages of pension planning and had simply instructed his clients what to do. It appeared that my rôle as an Independent Financial Adviser was just to help them to fill out the forms! Would that all transactions were that easy!

I returned to my office that evening feeling very fulfilled that a good job had been done. Nowadays, such is the burden of Regulation that the transaction would involve many hours of paperwork. Certainly, the process would probably involve two or three visits rather than just the one.

When the policy documents were produced by the Insurance Company, I delivered them personally. This, again, involved an overnight stay in an hotel. In no way did I begrudge the time or expense involved. I had, after all, earned by way of Commission my secretary's annual salary several times over.

John and Alan did exceptionally well, as predicted, and were soon employing twenty highly intelligent and skilful computer technicians. The business had moved from rather cramped offices and had acquired a beautiful but neglected manor house in the Somerset countryside from which to run their burgeoning enterprise. They set about restoring and extending to accommodate the growing number of experts under their control. When the work on the manor house was completed, they celebrated the grand opening with a Champagne reception at which Paddy Ashdown gave a stirring speech congratulating the Company on bringing so much employment to the area. At that time, they had about fifty employees and were fast becoming a force to be reckoned with in the South of England.

My friendly relationship with John and Alan grew with each visit. Each time they took on more staff members, I was summonsed to add them to the pension scheme. Each time I made a trip, I was assured of business of course. I made perhaps four or five visits a year. To thank them for the opportunity of helping them to make their Company grow, it became a habit to take the main directors out for lunch to a venue of their choice. I picked up the bill every time and was happy to do so. After all, these were my best clients, weren't they? This carried on for several years.

John had developed an interest in private flying and had acquired his Private Pilot's Licence. One day, I asked him if he would care to fly his light aircraft to my local airfield at Lydd in Kent. So it was that Alan and he came along to enjoy some Sussex hospitality for a change. This invitation they were happy to accept. Needless to say, I spared no expense and took them to the very best local hotel where we enjoyed a sumptuous meal at my expense before they flew back to Somerset.

One fateful day, I received a telephone call from Alan who said he had something to discuss with me. He asked me to visit their offices as usual. Something told me, however, that this proposed meeting was different from the normal ones. I sensed something sinister and was right to do so as it turned out.

"We enjoyed a sumptuous meal at my expense before they flew back to Somerset".

The Company had grown very substantially over the years and was now 100-strong. During that next meeting, it was explained to me that they had now outgrown my Company and felt that they were now of such a size and stature that they deserved to be advised by a major firm of Financial Advisers. As it happened, their new Finance Director had a brother who worked for such an organisation. A happy coincidence for them no doubt!

So it was that I returned home the next day with a heavy heart in the knowledge that the happy relationship which had grown between us had now come to an end.

When I broke the sad news to my Personal Assistant, her reaction surprised me. She suggested that I should regard the break as a happy release! She pointed out that the relationship had ceased to be profitable a long time ago. Of course, it had been very profitable in the early days but she was quite clear that all these trips up and down the motorways, all those lunches, bottles of Champagne at Christmas, birthday presents etc had to be measured against the income on each trip. The revenue from some of the trips was very modest but still my generosity kept on coming.

It was about then that I started to mature in business terms. Someone once said, "Turnover is vanity, profit is sanity". So true.

I suspect that few business owners are fortunate enough to be on a continually rising trajectory from Day One and throughout the existence of the enterprise. It is far more likely that the fortunes of an enduring business will rise and fall as lessons are learned and implemented. The experience I have described in this little anecdote epitomises an important lesson which I learned quite early on in the growth of my business. My Personal Assistant (who remained with me for sixteen years) was quite right to point out that my clients had long since ceased to be profitable. At the time, I remember feeling that she displayed a heartless side to her character but, in fact, she showed more business acumen than me in making that comment.

Retailers spend millions of pounds each year to calculate which products are creating the most profit for them. Those engaged in the selling of intangibles should do likewise. Lesson learned.

"Money can't buy happiness, but it can make you awfully comfortable while you're being miserable."

(Claire Luce)

— CHAPTER FIFTEEN —

Rich is Better

*A chance meeting with a local solicitor
- Aunty Rose and her millions
- A diversified investment put in place
- more income, more capital.*

Back in 1980, just before the first of our three boys was born, my wife and I attended an antenatal class in our local hospital. The main purpose of the class was for the nervous mums-to-be to learn how to breathe deeply and to relax. The expectant dads were there purely to lend support of course. Everyone was given a mattress which was placed upon the floor. As all this took place after work one evening, a few of the men simply dozed off. I am ashamed to admit that I was fast asleep in a few moments as was the man on the next mattress to mine. The two of us were a little embarrassed by the rest of the class when we awoke to their sniggers. It transpired that my exhausted friend was a local solicitor who, like me, was simply bushed after a hard day's work in the office. He and I struck up an acquaintanceship which has lasted to this day. James and I would often meet up for coffee or lunch. Such was the naturally suspicious nature of so many of those within the legal profession that it was many years later, after innumerable coffees or lunches (usually funded by me, I would add), that I received a call from James saying he wanted to see me about an important matter.

Accordingly, we met up in my office and he explained that his wife's aged aunt (recently widowed) needed some financial advice. This was the first time that he and I had ever spoken about a real live case together. Up until that point, James had only ever discussed with me the principals of investment or savings. I believe he had been testing me.

Anyway, it transpired that his wife's aunt, Mrs Rose Williams, had recently been widowed and had inherited her late husband's considerable fortune. He had been an employee of the same Insurance Company since he had left school, a period of fifty years or so. In his final thirty years, he had chosen to take his salary rises chiefly in the form of Company shares rather than in cash. It transpired that his confidence in the Company was completely justified. By the time of his death, the shares were riding high and had a value of over £4,000,000! This came as a bit of a shock for Aunty Rose. It appeared that, under the terms of the Will, she had the right to any income from the shares for her lifetime while the capital was to be left to a well-known Charity

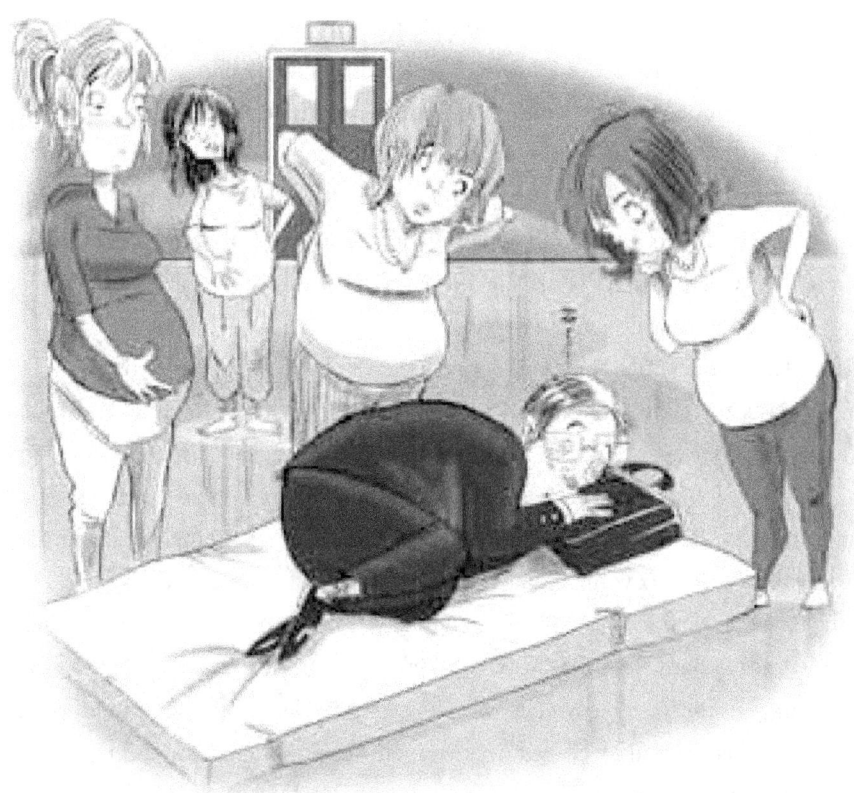

"I am ashamed to admit that I was fast asleep in a few moments".

following her eventual demise. James was acting as her solicitor and confidante. He had quite rightly recognised the dangers of Aunty Rose "having all her eggs in one basket" and was looking to me to help reduce the dependency of the bulk of her newly-swollen estate resting on the fortunes of just one Company. I fully concurred with the concept of diversifying her portfolio and set about doing just that. I drew up a proposition which spread her future risk between literally hundreds of enterprises around the globe. This was achieved by using collective (i.e. pooled) investment vehicles from different Investment Institutions. A substantial portfolio of Government Stock was also established for her.

The chief purpose of this strategy were to provide Aunty Rose with a highly tax-efficient and rising income into her remaining years and also to provide a hedge against the ravages of inflation for the capital which would eventually end up in the hands of the Charity. Incidentally, as the years progressed, the Insurance Company's fortunes took an almighty dive. Indeed, I recall calculating that, had the original shares remained in her possession, they would have lost millions and her income would have been vastly reduced as a result. Anyway, James agreed with my detailed proposals and accordingly, several weeks later, the new arrangements were put in place for her.

Aunty Rose and I met up every six months or so to review how the various investments were doing. We effected changes from time to time and took advantage of investment opportunities as they arose. I am pleased to say that in the years I looked after her affairs, Aunty Rose benefited from a rising income which far exceeded her expectations and requirements. Much of the surplus was given to young relatives who, it seemed to me, seldom gave her sufficient thanks for her extreme generosity. Furthermore, the capital itself rose to more than £5,500,000 which kept the Charity happy. Whether the huge responsibility of so much money ever sat easily on the shoulders of Aunty Rose is debatable. She always seemed to me to be consumed by worry about the whole thing despite the clear success of the strategy we had put in place for her. During our many meetings, she rarely smiled or gave any impression that she was pleased with the way things were going. In fact, it all appeared to be rather a burden for her as opposed to it being the Godsend which her late husband had no doubt intended for her. As I write this, Aunty Rose is now in her late 90s and I sincerely hope that her good fortune will continue for a few years yet and that it will give her some pleasure. After all, as Sophie Tucker is reputed to have said, "I've been rich and I've been poor. Rich is better."

Aunty Rose was one of wealthiest, luckiest and yet most generous women (generous, that is to her nieces and nephews) whom I have ever come across. She was also one of the most irascible, ungrateful and self-pitying souls whom I've ever met.

I regularly made the effort to go to see her - typically two or three times a year. The sole purpose of these meetings was to bring her up-to-date on the way the adopted strategy was working for her. Most times, I was able to show healthy growth and an increasing income. This news was generally met by silence or indifference. On occasions, inevitably, the markets had retreated since our previous meeting. This news was always met with great disappointment and criticism. The facts were clear, however. The arrangements I had put in place had increased the capital very substantially for the Charity and she had benefited from a rising income over the years. Mission accomplished!

"An investment in knowledge pays the best interest."

(Benjamin Franklin)

— CHAPTER SIXTEEN —

New Blood

The hunt for a new adviser - An extraordinary level of persistency pays off - There's no substitute for honesty.

In 1993, Shorter Byrne & Co set about finding another experienced sales person to advise clients and thus contribute towards the annual turnover figure which was already describing an upward trajectory thanks to the combined efforts of Robert Corbett , Clyde Young and John Shorter. John interviewed a large number of candidates over a period of weeks but few seemed to possess the attributes or qualities required.

One day, as John passed by his secretary's desk, he overheard her speaking rather curtly to someone on her telephone. He enquired of her to whom she had been talking. "Oh, it's just someone who keeps saying he wants to meet you. I am having some difficulty getting rid of him. He doesn't seem to take no for an answer". John asked how many times he had tried and this had apparently been the fourth occasion. Intrigued by this unusually persistent behaviour, John insisted that, should he call again, he should immediately be put through to him. The secretary had no contact details for the person involved.

Luckily, the very next day, he called once more. This time, John was put through to him and, following a brief conversation, invited him in to the office to have a meeting. It transpired that he had recently been made redundant from a second-tier Insurance Company and was really keen to join an Independent Financial Adviser firm and Shorter Byrne & Co in particular. The dogged determination which he had shown in making repeated attempts to get the appointment against all the odds was very impressive. This, John felt, could be the very man he had been searching for and the deal was struck.

Mark Holland had entered the financial world having successfully achieved a General Diploma in Business Studies which he passed with some distinction. His desire to remain up-to-date with contemporary thinking in the ever-changing world of financial services led to a further qualification in a Chartered Insurance Institute Examination.

Following a number of years with a major high street bank, during which time he rose to become a Supervisor of the Customer Care Department, Mark was then appointed to the position of Consultant with another well-respected financial institution. Finally, he was appointed Client Manager for the South East of England for the well-known Life Assurance, Investment and Pensions Company from whom he had just been made redundant along with many of his colleagues.

Mark always had a natural desire to be of genuine help to his clients. With his breadth of experience in the field of financial planning, together with the latest computer technology which was at his fingertips, he was well-placed to offer the high degree of care which the team was keen to extend to all its clients.

Because Mark was the youngest member of the team, he tended to identify with people of his own age. He therefore felt most comfortable dealing with people in their twenties and thirties. As he was consistently putting new younger clients on the books month by month, the inevitable effect was to reduce the average age of clients generally within the firm.

From Day One, Mark's natural, amiable and easy-going nature made him very popular with everyone within the firm. You couldn't help but like him and to appreciate the bonhomie which he projected. Clients found him very honest and approachable and it wasn't long before he began to make a substantial contribution to the growth of the firm. He remained very happily as an adviser within the firm for thirteen years until 2006.

A prerequisite of any person cast in the rôle of financial adviser is a natural sense of integrity and fair play. In the early days of his association with Mark, John saw evidence of Mark's honesty at first hand. They had attended a four-day shipboard conference together. One evening, during leisure time, Mark had met a couple of other advisers and they all went to the casino together. After a couple of hours, the others gave up and retired to their cabins but Mark continued on alone (persistency). At the beginning of the evening, Mark had suggested that any winnings should be equally shared (sense of fair play). He then got lucky on the blackjack table. The following morning, Mark deliberately sought out his companions from the previous evening to share his good fortune (honesty). Many people in that situation would have kept stum. If John had ever entertained any doubts about Mark's honesty, they disappeared at that point.

It has been said that you make your own luck. Mark gave us a good example of how to do it when he came back no fewer than five times to get what he wanted - an appointment. His level of determination was exceptional. Had he lost his temper or shown any kind of irritation to the secretary upon being rejected over and over, he would have lost the game. Once his "foot was in the door", however, his charm and gentle powers of persuasion took over. His belief in himself gave him the courage against all the odds.

"*The following morning, Mark deliberately sought out his companions from the previous evening to share his good fortune*".

Some Points to Ponder

Here follows a number of quotations which I have picked up from various people over the years. For some reason, each one has resonated with me.

"Don't confuse activity with profitability. Working harder will not help if your business is headed in the wrong direction. Leaders must be able to stop, think, and change what everyone is doing".

"Aim for the stars, and celebrate if you only land on the moon".

"If you want to be different, don't follow the crowd, choose your own route to success".

"If you want things to improve, it won't happen by continuing to do what you have previously been doing".

"If you are determined enough, you can make the impossible, possible".

"It doesn't matter what we think. What matters in the end is what we do".

"Young entrepreneurs are not experienced enough to be sensible, so they attempt the impossible – and achieve it, and keep on achieving it".

"You will never be shot at, if you don't stick your head above the parapet".

"To be a success you must be bold and be prepared to take a risk".

"If you want to find gold, you have got to be prepared to dig deep for it".

"If you can't find a way, hurry up and make your own way".

"Failure feeds winners. Winners learn from their mistakes and go on to become champions".

"You have a chance now to make sure that you do not die regretting what you could have, might have, or should have done. Live your life to the full now – tomorrow might never come"!

Keeping it Simple

Every interested party wants understandable solutions - investing versus depositing - get rich slow - watching out for the terrible Tax Trio - Trustworthy ongoing advice is key.

Over my 50-year career in financial services, I must have asked literally thousands of people what they were looking for from their ideal investment. Some people said they were seeking the maximum income they could obtain from their nest-egg. Others, being happily awash with surplus income from other sources, were far more interested in maximising capital growth for their future or that of their family. Everybody I spoke to justifiably required absolute security (i.e. protection against fraud) and the majority of people, when asked, admitted that they would prefer the strategy which was to be adopted for them to be SIMPLE.

In my view, it is to be applauded that the world of financial services has, through the medium of the press over the last few decades or so, been going out of its way to make the whole area of lump sum investment seem very much less mysterious than it previously appeared to be. The problem now seems to be that we are all suffering from a new disease: Information overload! The national newspapers and also television are bombarding us (especially at weekends) with a seemingly limitless range of differing ideas on how our precious capital could be invested.

Imagine for a wild moment that you have just learned that you are this week's Lottery Jackpot winner. Where are you going to go for advice to invest it? Some people would unhesitatingly put it on deposit in the High Street Building Society or Bank and will entertain a vague thought that they will probably do something "better" with it when they can get round to it. Others will speak to a firm of Stockbrokers to see what are recommend as the current "best buys". Still others, mindful of the dangers of ignoring the destructive effects of inflation upon deposited money over the long-term, would respond to those seductive newspaper advertisements which appear to them to offer the solution to their requirement for income or capital growth or both.

Yes, the whole world of investment does appear to be incredibly complex and dangerous to many people. Perhaps, that's the very reason for the phenomenal success of the Building Society movement in this country over so many years. People feel that the money will, at least, be safe there. Safe from what I wonder? Certainly not from the gradually erosive effects of inflation. Lottery winnings left in the high street Building Society into the years ahead could be likened to leaving a block of ice in the sun.

Even modest rates of inflation will certainly, if slowly, destroy its buying power bit by bit. Perhaps it's the comforting thought that Building Societies and Banks seldom collapse or run off with people's money, do they? ... and of course, it's a nice simple way of "investing". Actually, I'd prefer the term "depositing".

Giving the matter a little thought, most people would agree that investing a lump sum of money just cannot be as easy as merely asking which Building Society is paying the highest interest rate on a given day. If that were the case, why would the great investing institutions of this country, like pension funds and insurance companies, employ armies of investment managers, analysts and other experts to spread the billions of pounds of savers' money across all the world's stock markets, industrial and commercial property markets and money markets? The answer, of course, is that history shows us again and again that, given a reasonably continuous period of time, investing in real assets (as distinct from simply placing money on deposit) has always proved to be a successful antidote to the relatively modern phenomenon of inflation.

Making a decision on where to invest the monies however is only part of the problem. Another key issue is that of the TERRIBLE TAX TRIO - Income Tax, Capital Gains Tax and Inheritance Tax. It seems to me that there is little point to helping a client to build up a substantial amount of money for the next generation through highly successful investment strategies if no heed is taken of the Tax Man and the damage he can inflict. As an example, Inheritance Tax can snatch a pretty fair chunk of your estate away from your nearest and dearest if you fail to do anything about it. Because of the clever and effective mitigation schemes on offer from the ever-inventive Insurance Companies and other institutions, IHT could be referred to as a voluntary tax. Are these schemes simple enough for the ordinary person to understand? Generally speaking, people tend only to buy what they can understand.

An experienced and suitably-regulated Independent Financial Adviser is not only in a position to ascertain from you what your desires from the lump sum happen to be, but also to help you to select suitable financial products from the wide range available. To do this successfully, it is necessary to take careful account of information gleaned from you regarding your family circumstances, your short- and long-term requirements from the capital involved, your attitude towards investment volatility, your tax position and many other related matters. Therein lies the skill of the adviser. In brief, his (or, of course, her) responsibility is to express in as simple and straightforward a way as possible the advantages and disadvantages of the solutions which may be suitable in your particular case. Moreover, most Independent Financial Advisers worth their salt are keen to ensure that you are offered an ongoing service into the years ahead in order to ensure that any relevant changes in your circumstances or in the tax rules are taken into account within your chosen strategy and any relevant changes are swiftly put in hand.

Remember, a good Independent Financial Adviser will always KEEP IT SIMPLE!

Toptrak

*An invitation to join an elite group of advisers -
The open-handed sharing of ideas benefits all - The creation
of a well of accessible expertise for the benefit of clients.*

Many years ago I was one of hundreds of delegates who experienced a three-day intensive business conference on a magnificent P&O cruise liner. The meeting had been organised by PIMS (Personal Investment Marketing Show).

One evening, I found myself on deck with a glass of wine in hand. I got chatting to a very experienced and successful Independent Financial Adviser from the West Country, Richard Bateman. In the course of our discussions, we swapped sales and marketing ideas during a very agreeable couple of hours. As we parted, Richard enthusiastically suggested that I should attend the next quarterly meeting of a study group called Toptrak to which he belonged. This, he explained was an association of about twenty highly successful financial advisers who had been meeting on a regular basis to freely exchange transferable ideas and concepts for the benefit of clients and advisers alike. This whole idea appealed to me very much. For professional practitioners who are, after all, competitors in the same marketplace to pledge help and assistance to each other is very unusual in any other sphere of business.

I found my first meeting to be highly instructive and enjoyable. I had previously attended a handful of meetings in the past with other study groups over the years but had invariably found that they simply provided opportunities for prima donnas to show off! Toptrak was different. Great efforts were made to ensure that those who attended knew their stuff and had a reputation for working for the clients' benefit. They also had to be sincere in their desire to share with their fellow advisers. The highly organised meetings lasted from 9.00 a.m. to 5.00 p.m. and took place in the Dorchester Hotel in London's Park Lane. To make a full day of it, I usually made the effort to breakfast with some of the other 'early bird' Members at 8.00 a.m. As I had a (nearly) 2-hour door-to-door trip from my house, this necessitated a very early start but it was always well worth the effort. A sumptuous lunch was always provided in an adjoining room and the invited speakers from Insurance Companies and a mixture of other institutions joined us all for lunch and were generally of a very high calibre.

Meticulous Minutes would be e-mailed a day or two after the meetings by the highly efficient Toptrak Secretary and fellow member, Lee Clarke. These always served as a permanent reminder and reference point for the future. I remained an enthusiastic member of Toptrak for about twenty years until I retired.

Over the years of my Toptrak membership, many advisers from up and down the country were invited to attend a meeting, did so, and were never seen again. Membership was always by invitation only and, because priority was given to advisers with some original ideas, many invitees were simply judged to be not suitable as Members and were accordingly not invited to a second meeting. This strict ongoing vetting procedure resulted in a hardcore of regulars. Therein lay the secret of its success. Some of the Members were well-known figures within their area of expertise with some being eminent sought-after main platform speakers.

One of the many advantages of being involved with acknowledged experts in a particular field is that their specialist knowledge is a wonderful source of information when the situation presents itself. There were many occasions when I would find myself out of my depth on a particular subject when talking to a client. A telephone call or e-mail to a Member who happened to be suitably knowledgeable would then prove to be invaluable. It's not necessarily what you know...

"A dream written down with a date becomes a goal."

(Anon)

The Life Insurance Association and the Million Dollar Round Table

"It does not make sense to miss out on the chance to make new friends with likeminded individuals on both sides of the pond. Such friendships can, and do, last a lifetime".

When I first joined Abbey Life in 1972, I was very much aware that there was an atmosphere of excitement all around me within the Central London Branch which I had joined. There was a real sense of pioneering in the air. Most of the Agents (as we were called in those days) seemed to me to be larger than life and there were some real characters amongst them. There were about 80 of us if I recall correctly and our Branch Manager, Robert Sheridan, was much admired and held in high esteem by everyone. It was clear that he was a highly talented man of high principles and he insisted that every one of us always had the utmost integrity in all our dealings with clients. There was healthy competition to produce good quality business each month between our Branch and that of Langham Branch just down the road where the Branch Manager, Clive Holmes, presided.

I learned that the two men were good friends, held similar ideals, especially in the area of ensuring that education about financial services played an important part in our lives. Robert, Clive and a handful of others on the committee were instrumental in promoting the concept that the whole industry should be represented by a single body. A desire to upgrade the image of UK life assurance salespeople in the eyes of the public was the main driver and the ultimate goal was to have membership of the LIA widely recognised by the public as being synonymous with quality service. News of the fledgling association spread throughout all those involved in the selling of life assurance products and applications to join rolled in. Regionalised regular Meetings were organised and a superb magazine was produced on a monthly basis in which contributors throughout the land generously shared sales ideas and technical information. I used to look forward to receiving my Prospect magazine each month and, in particular, to enjoy being educated by the regular contributors and columnists some of whom were eminent in their field. The LIA grew very successfully over a number of years and in May 1993, Life Insurance Association Ireland became an autonomous body with the full support and encouragement of their colleagues in the UK. Great efforts were made to ensure that those involved in the giving of financial advice were suitably qualified by examination. This all helped to gradually convert the industry into a profession. For more than thirty years, the LIA was instrumental in improving the public's perception of those involved in financial advice.

Another organisation which many people within the Abbey Life office were aspiring to join was the Million Dollar Round Table (MDRT). Back in 1927, 32 highly successful life assurance producers met in Memphis, Tennessee. Their purpose was to meet together on a regular basis to benefit from sharing ideas and concepts with their peers. Founded on the belief that growth comes about as a result of the sharing of ideas, their mantra was "To receive, individuals must give".

To qualify, aspiring members had to prove that they had achieved a production level of $1,000,000 of face value permanent life assurance within the previous twelve months. This was a phenomenal amount of business at the time. The required production levels have been significantly changed over the years and became measured in commission and then in more recently, in commission/fees.

MDRT has now grown into a global independent association of more than 65,000 of the world's leading life assurance and financial services professionals from more than 500 companies in 70 nations. Members demonstrate exceptional professional knowledge, strict ethical conduct and outstanding levels of service for clients.

I attended my first four-day Annual Meeting in Radio City Music hall in New York. Along with thousands of others, I was highly impressed with the professional presentation and I learned ideas which I subsequently used to great effect over the years that followed. I became a Life Member of the MDRT having qualified for 25 consecutive years and each time I attended an Annual Meeting either in the USA or Canada, I was inspired by the best of the best within the profession. The quality of the inspirational speakers, many of whom were from outside the world of insurance, was just mind blowing and humbling. My one regret is that I did not attend more of the Annual Meetings.

Anyone within the profession who has achieved the requisite level of business should, in my view, definitely find out how to join. Not to do so would mean ignoring the opportunity to learn how to do a better job for ones clients and ultimately for oneself. Moreover, it does not make sense to miss out on the chance to make new friends with like-minded individuals on both sides of the pond. Such friendships can, and do, last a lifetime.

From Beginning to End

The History of the Shorter Byrne Partnership LLP

The Shorter Byrne Partnership LLP evolved over a 32-year span from a modest one-man business to a substantial and sophisticated financial planning firm where the main emphasis was on client loyalty.

The firm always tried to be at the forefront of developments within the retail sector of the rapidly-developing financial services industry. This chapter seeks to describe the history of the firm throughout its existence.

THE EARLY DAYS (1980 to 1988)

The Early Years 1980 to 1986

Following a number of happy and quite successful years in the field of direct selling, acting first as an agent for Abbey Life and then as a Sales Associate of Hambro Life, John Shorter made the decision, in March 1980, to start up an independent financial adviser practice. From the start, the practice was run on very strict lines to ensure that it avoided offending any regulations which were in existence at the time. An early application was therefore made to be enrolled under the regulations of the Insurance Brokers' Registration Council. Although it was not obligatory at that time, John Shorter decided that it would be prudent to have adequate Professional Indemnity Insurance in place from the word go.

The firm's turnover in its first year of operation was, by today's standards, tiny. The following year, (1981) showed a quantum leap, however, to a figure which doubled the previous year's performance. Then followed a further five years of healthy rises in turnover terms.

During that period, efforts were made to increase the public's awareness of the existence of the firm through a regular financial column in a local newspaper and the occasional local radio feature.

Years 1987 to 1988

It was at this time that a decision was made to bring another person on board to help develop the business by increasing sales volume, providing a broader spectrum of advice, offering the clients an alternative person to deal with in the event of illness or holidays etc. Since the very early years of the firm, RAC had been known to John Shorter in his capacity of a very reliable and knowledgeable Company Inspector from Standard Life. He certainly proved to be a very valuable addition to the firm at that time and, within 18 months or so, had helped push the turnover to double its previous highest level.

THE MIDDLE YEARS (1989 to 1997)

The previous two years had proved to be so successful in increasing turnover that it was considered perfectly feasible to try to repeat the exercise in 1989. Clyde Young, a senior management executive from a major unit-linked Insurance Company who had also been known to John Shorter for many years, was therefore accepted into the firm as an additional sales and marketing adviser. Whether the ensuing reduction in turnover which was suffered within 1989 and 1990 was caused through a enduring lack of investor confidence following the Stockmarket Crash at the end of 1987 or because of the time it took both RAC and John Shorter to help their new colleague 'up the ladder' is not clear. The fact is that the apparently relentless annual rise in turnover and profit which had been experienced without fail since 1980, faltered during 1989 and 1990.

However, whilst it is true to say that sales declined during those two years, it is also true that those were the very two years when some highly important radical decisions were made to effect a total change of emphasis within the business. There were two aspects to this. Firstly, thanks to the vision of Clyde Young, a great deal of effort was made to build up annual recurring "Renewal Fees" to create and enhance the actual value of the enterprise. A word of explanation here. Insurance Companies and other financial institutions rewarded the purveyors of their products in two ways. Firstly, by way of Initial Commission and secondly through far more modest Renewal Fees payable each year whilst the business remains on the books. Put another way, Initial Commission rewards the purveyor of the financial product for finding the client in the first place for and "putting the business on the books" whilst Renewal Fees represent the reward for keeping it there by providing a regular ongoing service to the client. As mentioned, the rate of Renewal Fees was tiny compared to Initial.

However, if every arranged policy, or investment, was structured to pay a smaller amount of Initial Commission plus an ongoing Renewal Fee each year, based on the value of the underlying investment, then all those amounts accumulate and can create a very significant and reliable source of income for the Financial Adviser and his company. It is that inbuilt income which, in time, becomes a highly attractive proposition from the point-of-view of an acquirer of the enterprise. There are two other key factors to taking this approach: (i) the ongoing Renewal Fee, being linked to the performance of the investment, makes the adviser and the client fully aligned i.e. they both have a vested interest in ensuring that a satisfactory investment performance is achieved over the long-term, and, (ii) the advisory practice that has a flow of ongoing "Renewal Fees" will benefit from that built-up income which, over time, will help to offset business expenses such as all staff salaries **before** a single product was sold. Geese and golden eggs come to mind!

Clyde Young's vision caused a radical change of thinking within the business but another change which came about was the introduction of a concept which was not only beneficial for the clients but which was also responsible for generating another layer of ongoing fee income. A system which Clyde and John dubbed "Daily Investment Monitoring" was introduced to all clients both existing and new. Under this arrangement, outside experienced experts in investment management were introduced to all relevant clients who had unit-linked policies. Thus, an additional element of care was brought to bear on policies where it was possible to vary the emphasis at minimal cost to the client from equities, Gilts, property and cash. Responsibility for the day-to-day management was therefore assumed by the investment experts and the clients were happy to pay for the service.

Yet another important decision was reached in 1989 and 1990. It was to put a great deal more effort into fostering business relationships with professional intermediaries. A handful of local Accountants and Solicitors had, from time to time, asked the firm to produce quotes for clients but there had been very little in the way of structured approaches made on the part of the firm over the years.

Accordingly, Clyde and John made a decision to offer a regular series of workshops and seminars especially geared to the requirements and for the interest of Accountants and Solicitors in equal measure. To facilitate inhouse seminars and to help to create an atmosphere conducive to attracting other professional intermediaries, it was decided to consider seriously seeking alternative office accommodation within the commercial hub of Eastbourne.

Years 1991 to 1992

The effort paid off surprisingly quickly. 1992 saw a doubling of turnover as against the previous year. It was also a record year for the firm.

In June 1991, John Shorter acquired the freehold premises of One Hyde Gardens and the business relocated as he had planned. The new prestigious offices, at the commercial epicentre of Eastbourne, almost immediately led to an increase in the number of enquiries from the local professional and business fraternity as well as a regular number of unsolicited general enquiries from the public at large.

Years 1993, 1994 and 1995

During these three years, the Financial Services world had been characterised by huge changes in legislation, Regulatory pressures and a general mistrust on the part of the public. Nonetheless, Shorter Byrne & Co (as they were known in those days) witnessed a 16% increase in turnover.

Due to the increasing pressures upon John Shorter to produce business each month, to keep on top of Compliance issues and to devote time to forward planning and development, it was decided in 1993 to take on a new sales person. Several candidates were considered and Mark Holland was finally engaged.

His first few years of performance in terms of Initial Commission and Fundbased Fee Income proved that the right man had been chosen and his figures showed a dramatic and regular year-on-year improvement.

He remained a consistent producer of good quality business and proved himself to be a very valuable and reliable member of the team. The success which Mark enjoyed in his early business life in advising the public on financial planning matters such as family life assurance protection, regular savings plans, ISAs etc meant that he had tended to identify with people of his own age. This in turn had lowered the average age of clients within the Company thus ensuring a healthy continuity of business from that quarter into the future.

In 1994, after careful consideration and encouraged by excellent profits (considering a countrywide recessional decline), Shorter Byrne & Co made a commercial decision to introduce office-wide automation and accordingly invested a substantial amount into computer technology. A fully integrated network was installed thus placing a PC on the desk of every member of staff. This dramatically enhanced the types of service offered to its clients and put the firm in a very good position to handle yet greater volumes of business.

In April 1995, a radical decision was taken to engage the services of a Practice Development Manager on a substantial salary.

His rôle was to concentrate upon all issues connected with the ever-increasing burden of Compliance; to deal with all matters to do with secretarial support; to help wherever possible to foster relationships with a number of existing professional connections; to stimulate fresh relationships with local Accountants and Solicitors of his acquaintance; to create and maintain a regular information communication service for existing and prospective clients; to ensure the smooth running of the office and a host of other associated responsibilities.

It became obvious that, with the growing importance of Compliance issues, a greater emphasis would have to be placed on that specific area. As mentioned earlier, from the very beginning, the firm had always resolved to adhere to whatever rules and regulations prevailed. With this in mind, a decision was made to engage the services of a top quality Office Manager (Marilyn) whose job it would be to oversee the day-to-day activities of the growing administration staff but leave Compliance issues entirely in the hands of a dedicated individual.

THE NEXT EIGHT YEARS (1998 to 2006)

Years 1998 to 2006

With all administrative and staff matters now safely in the capable hands of the Office Manager, a search once more was instigated, to find a fulltime experienced Compliance Officer. John Shorter quickly identified an individual who for many years had been a highly-skilled and knowledgeable Director of a City-based national IFA Company. Not only did he have a great deal of experience in the area of Compliance but he also had the potential to bring an investment-oriented client base to the party. He was initially engaged on a temporary consultancy basis. However, after a matter of weeks, it became obvious that the firm would benefit enormously from his expertise and he was accordingly offered a permanent employed position which he readily accepted. He, in turn, almost immediately introduced a highly successful colleague from his old Company in the City whose speciality was pension planning in the individual and corporate arena. His ex-colleague was therefore also engaged as a further employed Registered Individual with a specific brief to expand individual and corporate Group Pensions business within the firm. Once more, having this new individual as part of the expanded team was not only going to be an attractive proposition because of his proven and specialist skills, as evidenced by his coveted pension qualification (G60), but he too was in a position to bring with him a substantial and mature client base. This indeed came about.

The addition of these two high quality experts in their fields allowed John Shorter to realise a vision which he had long held of creating a Limited Company environment which would eventually become a highly profitable and therefore valuable asset for the future. When he judged the moment was right, therefore, he proposed that Shorter Byrne & Co should incorporate and he therefore offered the opportunity to his three colleagues to become Shareholding Directors of the newly-formed Company. In due course, therefore, a Shareholders' Agreement was drawn up by a City-based firm of lawyers and Shorter Byrne & Co Ltd was accordingly born on the first day of the new millennium on 1st January 2000.

The growth of Shorter Byrne & Co and the Limited Company both in terms of turnover and manpower during its twenty-year history up till that point was consistent and considerable, spanning as it did a period which was fraught with political and economic uncertainties both in the UK and worldwide.

It was during the difficult years (i.e. 1989 and 1990) described earlier that the important aspect of bottom line profit rather than mere turnover took on a crucially important meaning for the firm. Who was it who once said, "Turnover is vanity, profit is sanity"?

It was predicted that the healthy and sustainable growth of profits experienced for so many years would continue into the years ahead especially as the strategic plans which were continuously laid down paid dividends.

However, after the new limited company was born, John Shorter couldn't help noticing that an ever-increasing amount of his time was having to be spent on such tasks as improving office systems, perfecting administration protocols, observing directorial duties, following Regulatory guidelines and so many other activities which, although important, were in no way connected with the activity of advising or helping clients. An insidious change had been creeping in to adjust the way he was spending his time day-to-day and it seemed to be getting worse. He set about monitoring the amount of time being devoted to actually advising clients and discovered to his surprise and disappointment that the time being spent with clients accounted for between 5% to 10% of his working day. He asked himself the question whether he wanted to continue on the course of being an increasingly busy office-bound administrator. It did not take long to remind himself that the most enjoyable and fulfilling part of being an adviser was interacting with and providing help to actual clients to navigate the complex area of financial planning.

By then, the Company had grown to a total of fourteen employees, four Directors and about two thousand four hundred clients – many of whom inevitably fell into the category of "historical product purchasers". The daily demands upon John Shorter's time meant that there was very little opportunity left to spend time with clients. Following some very serious thought, the major decision was therefore made to split the Company up and for the four Directors to go their separate ways.

This was effected in a very controlled and gentlemanly way with clients being allocated to each Director so that, from the clients' perspective, it was a seamless process. This resulted in a small number of clients, about 100, continuing to be looked after by John Shorter personally. Thus the transformation took place.

THE FINAL YEARS (2006 to 2012)

On 1st July 2006, John Shorter therefore started an exciting new enterprise - The Shorter Byrne Partnership LLP. John's wife, Vivienne, joined the firm and the much reduced staff. In previous years, her involvement with the business had always been a supporting one from the family home but she immediately took to the work and enjoyed the day-to-day running of the smaller operation. Her involvement with clients was an important rôle and her friendly nature and unwavering desire to be of help paid great dividends.

For the previous twenty odd years, the emphasis within the firm had always been to provide the very highest possible level of service and care to all its clients. This determination to provide the best level of care to everyone always becomes a real challenge, however, as the number of clients under ones charge increases. This newly-formed enterprise was able to maintain a high quality of service only because the number of clients then being looked after had been considerably reduced from the previous levels.

With any well-established Company, once a large number of clients has been 'put on the books', it is inevitable that some will fall into the category of "historical product purchasers". As has been explained, the number of clients being looked after by John Shorter had been deliberately pared down to about 100. Great efforts were made each year to ensure that all clients continued to feel important and cared about.

For many years, the professional expertise of specially-selected third party fund managers (the investment experts) had been harnessed for the benefit of all investment clients. This extra level of service whereby a system of Daily Investment Monitoring had been brought to bear upon the savings of clients had been very well received and appreciated by clients. This was evidenced by the fact that the additional fees being charged for the service continued to be voluntarily paid by clients year-on-year. The crucial rôle of the fund managers was to ensure, as far as is possible, that clients' money was in the right place at the right time. Due emphasis was placed upon the importance of UK and Overseas equities, Industrial and Commercial Property, Government Stock, Cash Deposits and so on as the different cycles dictated.

Similarly, in the area of Long-Term Care planning and equity release, outside experts were called on for their specialist advice for the benefit of clients showing an interest in those subjects.

Personal and corporate financial planning became so sophisticated and complex that a small firm of Independent Financial Advisers found it challenging to say the least to ensure that the very best of contemporary advice was being given at all times to all clients. In the medical world, your GP will often refer his patients to a specialist when warranted. It is a system which has worked well for a very long time. In exactly the same way, the firm believed that their rôle in financial services was to ensure that all clients' needs were catered for properly and professionally. If that meant calling in an outside expert who possessed the appropriate qualifications and experience to handle the matter correctly, then they were happy to do so. In fact, they had gathered around themselves over the years an elite team of specialists with whom they had an excellent relationship and in whom they had the utmost faith that their ethos and integrity matched their own.

They were constantly on the lookout for outstanding expertise in the marketplace and were keen to expand their team of experts if and when the right individuals could be identified. This was an ongoing process to ensure that they were always in a position to have their clients' financial problems referred to the best brains available in the market.

A regular informative newsletter was posted out free-of-charge to all clients as well as to a large number of people who were yet to become clients and, of course, to all the professional connections such as Solicitors and Accountants.

On the subject of professional connections, the series of regular workshops and seminars which was initiated back in the late eighties by John Shorter and Clyde Young continued. These had always been very popular and had been very well-attended. There is no doubt that they did much to cement the personal relationships between the firm and the local Solicitors, Accountants, Insurance Brokers, Stockbrokers etc. The spin-off benefits of making the effort to run such seminars continued to be considerable. John Shorter was asked by a local Solicitor to be a guest speaker on Inheritance Tax mitigation at the prestigious Society of Trust and Estate Practitioners.

This led to a number of excellent new relationships being formed and some very substantial new enquiries which helped to boost the reputation and income of the Firm by a considerable margin.

The volatile and miserable global investment conditions which prevailed for much of the past decade left many IFAs wondering if the lack of interest of potential new investors would ever come to an end. The Shorter Byrne Partnership LLP, by comparison, thankfully experienced no such slackening off of business. On the contrary, these proved to be very busy years. The firm always took pains to ensure that all their clients recognised that the greatest opportunities for investment arise during such seemingly hopeless times. This educative process offered great rewards and helped to ensure that the blank periods, which dog so many small IFA Companies, did not materialise.

Despite the fact that the firm, now much reduced in size, seemed to be going from strength to strength, the daily effort required to keep the show on the road was beginning to tell. More importantly, John Shorter was acutely aware of his age and the fact that the years were marching on. It seemed to him that the time was fast approaching when it would make sense to bring a long career to a gentle conclusion. For some years, he had considered the sage words of Logan Pearsall Smith: "There are two things to aim at in life: first, to get what you want; and after that, to enjoy it. Only the wisest of people achieve the second." It was time to travel more and further afield, catch some more salmon, collect more antiques, turn wood and play the saxophone - all much-loved pursuits which hitherto had always been made to take second place to the business.

In 2012, some 32 years after its inception, and in John Shorter's 65th year, a younger man, a reliable and very honest buyer was found for the firm. Retirement, something which had always been at the back of his mind, actually came to fruition for John Shorter. It was then that the deliberate effort which had been made back in the 1990s to create a saleable value for the business came at last to fruition.

Some useful Ideas

The handful of sales aids to be found on the pages which follow were found to be very useful in all kinds of situations with clients. They represent some of my favourites and they were always to be found in my briefcase. To avoid them becoming worn or dog-eared, each one was plasticised. Once I had become totally familiar with each one, I would immediately select whichever one was relevant to the situation which was being discussed with the client - much like a juke-box will select a record! The written word becomes very powerful and is seldom questioned.

WARNING

As I write this book, I have already been retired for nearly ten years. If anyone in financial services is aiming to use any of these ideas, they should first ensure with the relevant body that they comply with any regulations which may have come into effect during this interim period. I have endeavoured to ensure that I have selected only those ideas which have stood the test of time and which convey valuable messages irrespective of the time in which they are used. For this exercise, I have avoided any which have a "sell-by date". It has been said that there are no new ideas but that new ones are simply interpretations of old ones. I have always tried to create fresh and unique concepts but have to admit that some might have been inspired by previous ideas from others.

Descriptions of Sales Aids and How They Can be Used

The Six Golden Rules of Investment

One day, I asked my co-Directors to join me in writing down the sayings or expressions which they found to be highly effective in getting a point across to clients. I then selected just six which I felt had particular merit. I then had them illuminated on vellum by an artist. The result was then framed and hung in the clients' meeting room in a gilded frame.

How it can be used

During meetings, from time to time, clients would say, for example, that their investments had been behaving in a disappointing fashion and that their money would have been better off in a Building Society.

I would then look at the Six Rules on the wall, and pointing to them, would say, "Ah yes. You mean Rule No 5 don't you?". Somehow, that always helped to put matters in perspective.

The Six Golden Rules of Investment

1. Remember that this is a "get rich slow" system!

2. Don't forget that the people who benefit most over the long-term from your depositing money in the Building Society are the ones who go in there to borrow it.

3. Realise that investing in the world's great commercial enterprises over the long-term does make sense.

4. Always remember that equities, like roller coasters, can go down as well as up!

5. Do not be tempted to tell us that you would be better off back in the Building Society - it will only be a temporary phenomenon.

6. Having made this investment for the medium to long-term, please do not be tempted to keep digging up the seeds to see how they're doing!

Respectfully suggested by Shorter Byrne & Co. Ltd.

A Point to Ponder

I learned somewhere that the Chinese word for "Risk" was comprised of two characters and that each one had its own separate meaning. I went to the Chinese Embassy in London to find out more. What you see is what I found out.

How it can be used

This made it crystal clear to the "risk averse" clients that there are actually two sides to the story.

A POINT TO PONDER …

The Chinese character for the word "RISK" is :

Please note that the first part means DANGER
whilst the second part means OPPORTUNITY !

THE SHORTER BYRNE PARTNERSHIP LLP
INDEPENDENT FINANCIAL ADVISERS
One Hyde Gardens, Eastbourne, East Sussex BN21 4PN
Telephone: (01323) 725624 Fax: (01323) 410430
The Shorter Byrne Partnership LLP is an Appointed Representative of Investment & Tax Advisory Services Limited
which is authorised and regulated by the Financial Services Authority

The World's Stockmarkets & their relative sizes

In an effort to encourage clients to diversify their investments, I found it beneficial to point out that the UK Stockmarket, although important, should always be put into perspective.

How it can be used

Whenever clients made it clear to me that, in their view, the UK Stockmarket (as measured by the FTSE-100 Index) was just a synonym for stocks and shares or equities, I would show them this to make it clear that other opportunities exist outside our shores.

THE WORLD'S STOCKMARKETS & THEIR RELATIVE SIZES

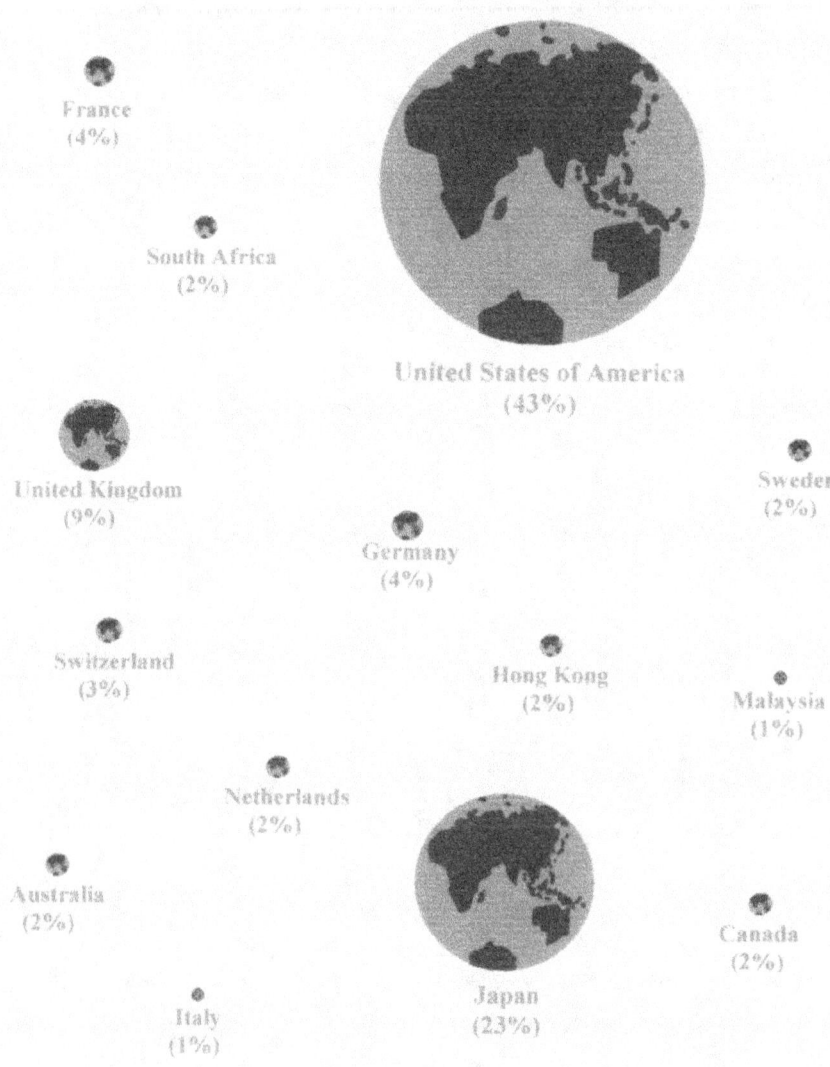

The Law of Diminishing Concerns

Isn't it strange that what appears to be a total disaster today becomes less and less of a problem as time passes. This is true in all aspects of life - notably in the field of investment.

How it can be used

Clients who are inexperienced in investment matters often say that because of the dramatic drops in value which occur from time to time in the Stockmarket, they would not want to get involved. One such "crash" involved a particularly serious fall in values in July 2011. Now see it against a backdrop of 1 year, 2 years, 5 years and finally, 25-year periods.

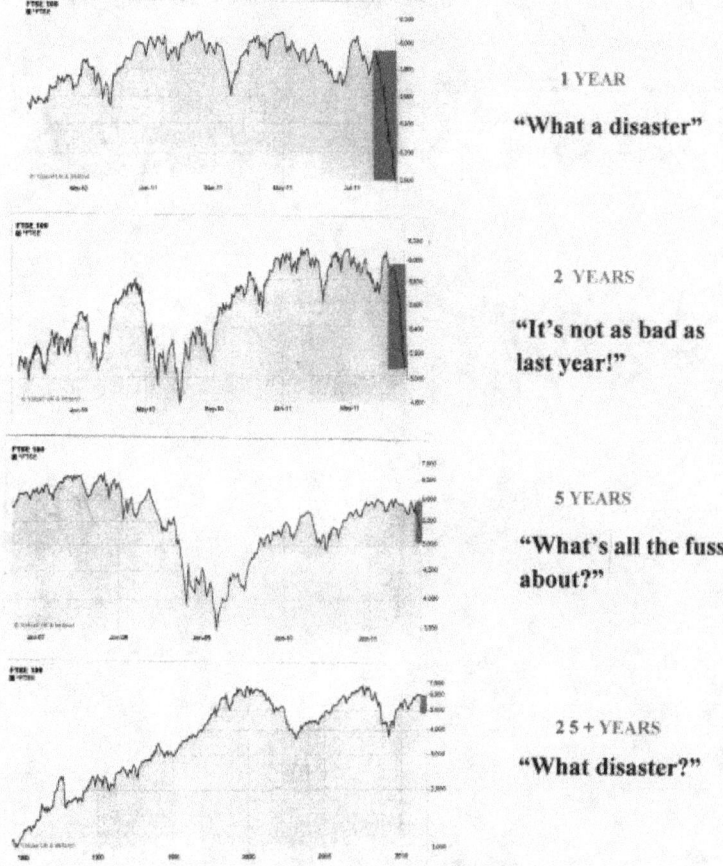

The Wonderful Rule of 72

This is a particularly useful tool. Such a simple and yet effective way of calculating, in an instant, the number of years a figure will double or halve taking an assumed rate into account.

How it can be used

All you have to do is to remember the number 72! Knowledge of this simple formula will do nothing but enhance your image in front of your clients. For example...

Client: *How long will it take for my invested capital to double in value?*
You: *At an assumed annual growth rate of 5%, it will take about 14 years but, at 6%, 12 years should do it.*

 # THE WONDERFUL RULE OF 72

Question 1:

How long would it take for a sum of money to double in size if it accumulated with growth of say 5% per annum?

Answer: 14 years

Question 2:

How long would it take for the real value of a sum of money to halve assuming an inflation rate of say 3% per annum?

Answer: 24 years

It's simple. Just divide 72 by the growth/inflation rate assumed. It works every time!

The Magic of Compound Growth

Very recently, I heard of a client who had been "advised" by his IFA that he was too young at 38 to be bothered with starting to save for a pension. I can only imagine that the IFA must have been off ill when they were teaching about the benefit of compounding!

How it can be used

This little presentation shows that the longer the delay before starting the savings process, the greater the monthly contribution must be to achieve the objective. The opposite is also true in that, the earlier you start, the less you have to contribute overall and the easier the journey becomes.

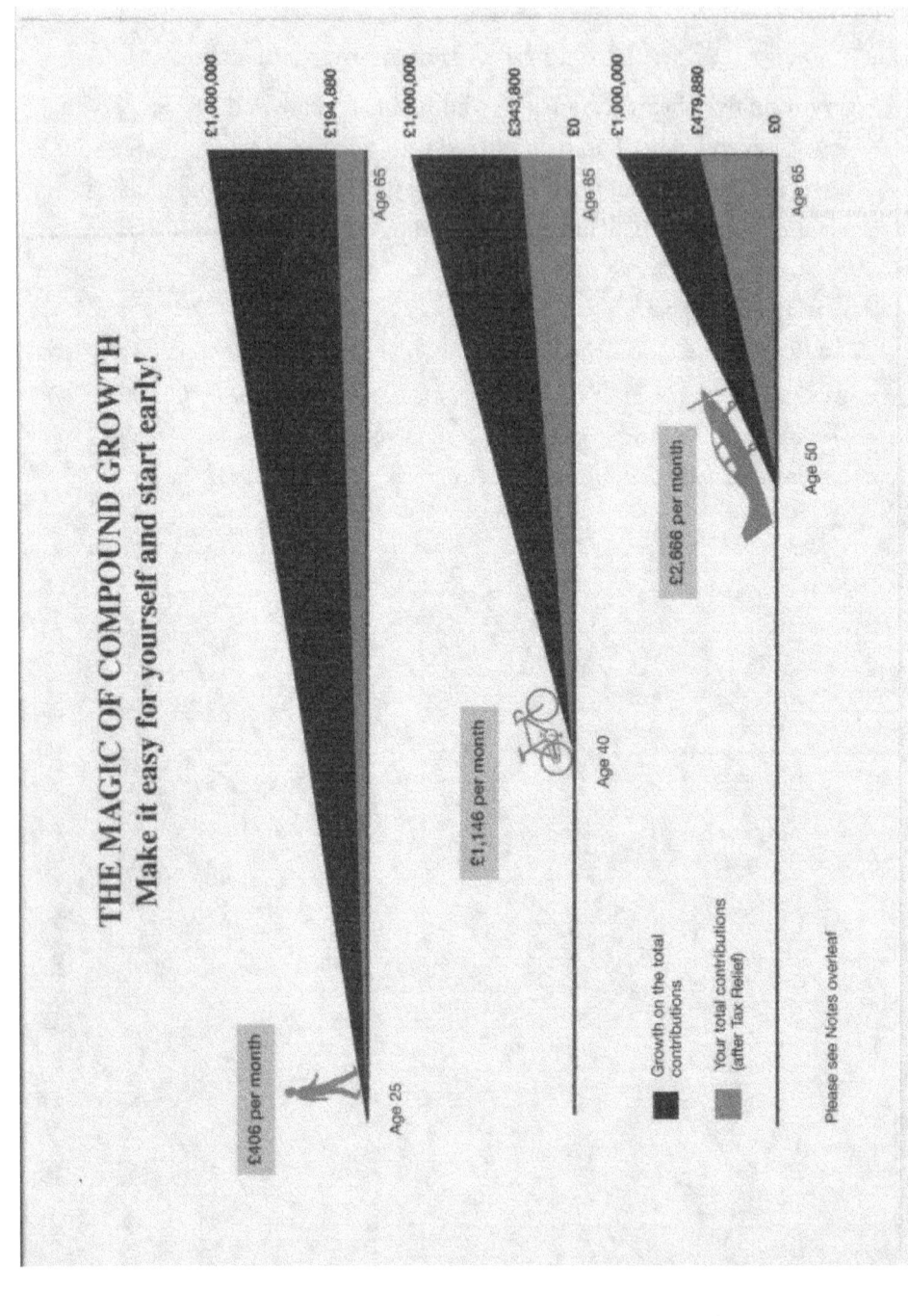

Why You Should Start Saving NOW

This presentation tells a similar story to the previous one (The Magic of Compound Growth). The advantage of starting to save early is clear but it also shows that the power of compounding means that, if desired, the saving could stop at the 10-year point and compounding will do the rest.

How it can be used

The client can be given the choice of either starting now and saving for just 10 years (Method A) or delaying the start but saving for 20 years (Method B). The first way produces a result which is 30% higher!

WHY YOU SHOULD START SAVING NOW

(or "Use compound growth to your advantage!")

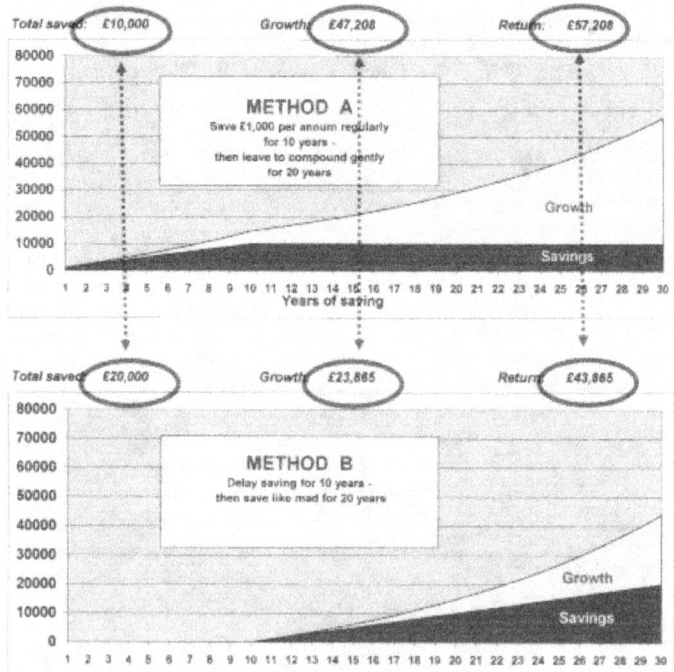

Suggestion : Use Method A rather than Method B

Reasons:
1. You save half as much

2. Your investment works much harder

3. You finish up with MUCH MORE money!

Please remember that past performance is not necessarily a guide to future performance. You may not get back all that you have invested. An assumed growth rate of 7% per annum has used been throughout the calculations.
The above is intended to be helpful and is not based upon the experience of any particular investor.

THE SHORTER BYRNE PARTNERSHIP LLP
INDEPENDENT FINANCIAL ADVISERS
One Hyde Gardens, Eastbourne, East Sussex BN21 4PN
Telephone 01323 725624 Fax: 01323 410439 e-mail johnshorter@shorterbyrne.co.uk
The Shorter Byrne Partnership LLP is an Appointed Representative of Investment & Tax Advisory Services Limited
which is authorised and regulated by the Financial Services Authority

A Dire Warning

I came across these very wise words from John Ruskin (leading philosopher and prominent social thinker of the Victorian Age) and immediately thought how they could be applied in all kinds of situations in life today.

How it can be used
If a client offers the opinion that a charge or fee is excessive, a quick run through these sage words should do the trick!

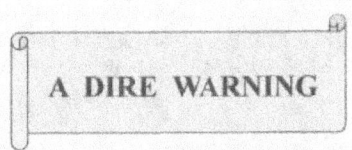

It's unwise to pay too much, but it's worse to pay too little. When you pay too much you lose a little money - that is all. When you pay too little, you sometimes lose everything because the thing you bought was incapable of doing the thing it was bought to do.

The common law of business balance prohibits paying a little and getting a lot - it can't be done. If you deal with the lowest bidder, it is well to add something for the risk you run. And if you do that, you will have enough to pay for something better.

John Ruskin - 1819 - 1900

For 100 Young People Today...

At first glance, this looks like a rather depressing outlook for most young people doesn't it? Presented in the right way, however, it should encourage people with the right attitude to ensure that they do everything possible to avoid poverty in retirement.

How it can be used

When a prospective client has made it clear that they have a desire to retire at 65, for example, this warning of what might lie ahead offers a powerful incentive to ensure that they will do everything possible to succeed in doing so with dignity.

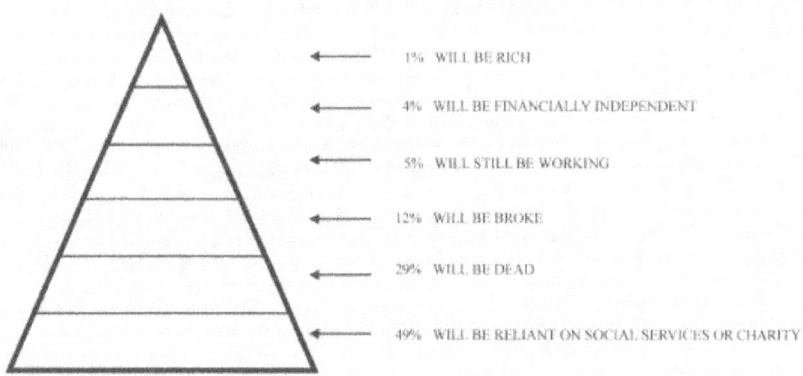

FOR 100 YOUNG PEOPLE TODAY NOW AGED 25, THIS COULD BE THE PICTURE AT RETIREMENT IN 40 YEARS' TIME

- 1% WILL BE RICH
- 4% WILL BE FINANCIALLY INDEPENDENT
- 5% WILL STILL BE WORKING
- 12% WILL BE BROKE
- 29% WILL BE DEAD
- 49% WILL BE RELIANT ON SOCIAL SERVICES OR CHARITY

PUT ANOTHER WAY, OF THOSE WHO LIVE UNTIL RETIREMENT, 93% WILL BE EITHER STILL WORKING OR DEPENDENT ON EITHER THE GOVERNMENT OR ON FRIENDS, RELATIVES OR CHARITY

Approximate Monthly Contributions...

This is a very handy ready reckoner to keep in your briefcase at all times.

How it can be used

If it has been established with your client that a target sum of money will be needed at some point in the future, this reckoner makes it very quick and easy to see what the monthly commitment has to be to achieve it. For example, £100,000 in 10 years' time at an assumed annual growth rate of 6% will require a monthly of £659. Easy peasy.

APPROXIMATE MONTHLY CONTRIBUTIONS TO PRODUCE A GIVEN FIGURE OVER 5 to 25 YEARS

	5 Yrs			10 Yrs			15 Yrs			20 Yrs			25 Yrs		
	6%	9%	12%	6%	9%	12%	6%	9%	12%	6%	9%	12%	6%	9%	12%
£5,000	£74	£69	£63	£33	£28	£24	£19	£15	£11	£13	£9	£6	£9	£5	£3
£10,000	£148	£137	£126	£66	£56	£47	£39	£30	£23	£26	£18	£12	£18	£11	£7
£15,000	£223	£206	£190	£99	£84	£71	£58	£45	£34	£39	£27	£18	£27	£17	£10
£20,000	£297	£274	£253	£132	£112	£94	£78	£60	£46	£51	£36	£24	£36	£23	£14
£25,000	£371	£343	£316	£165	£140	£118	£97	£75	£57	£64	£45	£31	£45	£28	£17
£30,000	£445	£411	£379	£198	£168	£141	£117	£90	£69	£77	£54	£37	£54	£34	£21
£35,000	£519	£480	£442	£231	£195	£165	£136	£105	£80	£90	£63	£43	£63	£40	£24
£40,000	£593	£548	£505	£264	£223	£188	£155	£120	£91	£103	£72	£49	£72	£45	£27
£45,000	£668	£617	£569	£297	£251	£212	£175	£135	£103	£116	£81	£55	£81	£51	£31
£50,000	£742	£685	£632	£329	£279	£235	£194	£150	£114	£128	£90	£61	£90	£57	£34
£55,000	£816	£754	£695	£362	£307	£259	£214	£165	£126	£141	£99	£67	£99	£62	£38
£60,000	£890	£822	£758	£395	£335	£282	£233	£180	£137	£154	£108	£73	£108	£68	£41
£65,000	£964	£891	£821	£428	£363	£306	£253	£195	£148	£167	£117	£80	£117	£74	£45
£70,000	£1,039	£959	£884	£461	£391	£329	£272	£210	£160	£180	£126	£86	£126	£79	£48
£75,000	£1,113	£1,028	£948	£494	£419	£353	£291	£225	£171	£193	£135	£92	£135	£85	£51
£80,000	£1,187	£1,096	£1,011	£527	£447	£376	£311	£240	£183	£206	£144	£98	£144	£91	£55
£85,000	£1,261	£1,165	£1,074	£560	£475	£400	£330	£255	£194	£218	£153	£104	£153	£96	£58
£90,000	£1,335	£1,233	£1,137	£593	£503	£423	£350	£270	£206	£231	£162	£110	£162	£102	£62
£95,000	£1,410	£1,302	£1,200	£626	£531	£447	£369	£285	£217	£244	£170	£116	£171	£108	£65
£100,000	£1,484	£1,370	£1,263	£659	£559	£470	£389	£300	£229	£257	£179	£122	£180	£113	£69
£105,000	£1,558	£1,439	£1,327	£692	£586	£494	£408	£315	£240	£270	£188	£129	£189	£119	£72
£110,000	£1,632	£1,507	£1,390	£725	£614	£517	£427	£330	£251	£282	£197	£135	£198	£125	£75
£115,000	£1,706	£1,576	£1,453	£758	£642	£541	£447	£345	£263	£295	£206	£141	£207	£130	£79
£120,000	£1,780	£1,644	£1,516	£791	£670	£564	£466	£360	£274	£308	£215	£147	£216	£136	£82
£125,000	£1,855	£1,713	£1,579	£824	£698	£588	£486	£375	£286	£321	£224	£153	£225	£142	£86
£130,000	£1,929	£1,781	£1,642	£857	£726	£611	£505	£390	£297	£334	£233	£159	£234	£147	£89
£135,000	£2,003	£1,850	£1,706	£890	£754	£635	£525	£405	£308	£347	£242	£165	£243	£153	£93
£140,000	£2,077	£1,918	£1,769	£922	£782	£658	£544	£420	£320	£359	£251	£171	£252	£159	£96
£145,000	£2,151	£1,987	£1,832	£955	£810	£682	£563	£435	£331	£372	£260	£177	£261	£164	£99
£150,000	£2,226	£2,055	£1,895	£988	£838	£705	£583	£450	£343	£385	£269	£183	£270	£170	£103
£155,000	£2,300	£2,124	£1,958	£1,021	£866	£729	£602	£465	£354	£398	£278	£190	£279	£176	£106
£160,000	£2,374	£2,192	£2,021	£1,054	£894	£752	£622	£480	£365	£411	£287	£196	£288	£181	£110
£165,000	£2,448	£2,261	£2,085	£1,087	£922	£776	£641	£495	£377	£424	£296	£202	£297	£187	£113
£170,000	£2,522	£2,329	£2,148	£1,120	£949	£799	£661	£510	£388	£436	£305	£208	£306	£193	£117
£175,000	£2,597	£2,398	£2,211	£1,153	£977	£823	£680	£525	£400	£449	£314	£214	£315	£198	£120
£180,000	£2,671	£2,466	£2,274	£1,186	£1,005	£846	£699	£540	£411	£462	£323	£220	£324	£204	£123
£185,000	£2,745	£2,535	£2,337	£1,219	£1,033	£870	£719	£555	£423	£475	£332	£226	£333	£210	£127
£190,000	£2,819	£2,603	£2,400	£1,252	£1,061	£893	£738	£570	£434	£488	£341	£232	£342	£215	£130
£195,000	£2,893	£2,672	£2,464	£1,285	£1,089	£917	£758	£585	£445	£501	£350	£239	£351	£221	£134
£200,000	£2,967	£2,740	£2,527	£1,318	£1,117	£940	£777	£600	£457	£513	£359	£245	£360	£227	£137

NB An Annual Management Charge of 1.50% has been assumed

Expectation of Life Table

This information is readily available and should, in my view, always form part of the armoury of anyone involved in advising on financial services.

How it can be used

This table can be useful in all sorts of situations. The young lady of 30, for instance, has over 50 years of life on average ahead of her according to the table. If she has stated a desire to retire at age 60, for example, a glance at this table shows that she may have nearly 24 or more retirement years.

EXPECTATION OF LIFE TABLE

Expectation of life (in years)

Current age	Males	Females	Current age	Males	Females
20	57.35	61.54	60	20.49	23.64
21	56.39	60.56	61	19.69	22.78
22	55.42	59.57	62	18.90	21.93
23	54.46	58.59	63	18.14	21.09
24	53.51	57.61	64	17.38	20.26
25	52.64	56.62	65	16.63	19.44
26	51.59	55.64	66	15.89	18.63
27	50.63	54.66	67	15.17	17.84
28	49.67	53.68	68	14.46	17.05
29	48.70	52.70	69	13.77	16.27
30	47.75	51.72	70	13.09	15.51
31	46.79	50.74	71	12.42	14.75
32	45.83	49.77	72	11.78	14.02
33	44.88	48.79	73	11.16	13.30
34	43.93	47.81	74	10.55	12.60
35	42.97	46.84	75	9.97	11.92
36	42.02	45.87	76	9.41	11.26
37	41.08	44.90	77	8.87	10.63
38	40.13	43.93	78	8.36	10.01
39	39.18	42.97	79	7.86	9.41
40	38.24	42.00	80	7.39	8.83
41	37.30	41.04	81	6.95	8.28
42	36.37	40.08	82	6.52	7.75
43	35.43	39.13	83	6.12	7.24
44	34.51	38.18	84	5.73	6.75
45	33.58	37.24	85	5.35	6.27
46	32.66	36.29	86	4.98	5.82
47	31.75	35.26	87	4.63	5.40
48	30.84	34.42	88	4.34	5.02
49	29.94	33.50	89	4.07	4.67
50	29.04	32.58	90	3.82	4.34
51	28.16	31.66	91	3.57	4.02
52	27.28	30.75	92	3.33	3.73
53	26.40	29.84	93	3.11	3.46
54	25.53	28.93	94	2.92	3.22
55	24.67	28.04	95	2.71	3.00
56	23.82	27.14	96	2.55	2.80
57	22.97	26.26	97	2.40	2.62
58	22.13	25.38	98	2.26	2.45
59	21.30	24.50	99	2.14	2.30

Source: Government Actuary's Department – May 2007

NB The above figures are based on the mid-year population estimates for 2003, 2004 & 2005 and corresponding data on births, infant deaths and deaths by individual age from those years.

The Conclusion

Whether you are in financial services or in some other trade or profession, I sincerely hope that you might have discovered something, just something, within these pages which will prove to be of value in your quest for success and fulfilment.

I have tried to give you an insight into how my particular career progressed and have done so in the hope that you may be able to identify with some of the situations which I have described.

You may have noticed that I have dedicated this book to our three sons, Giles, Jerome and Alexander. As I have mentioned elsewhere in these pages, they are now each successful entrepreneurs in their own right. None of them, of course, experienced success from Day One. It tends not to work like that. They earned their success by doggedly going through the unavoidable stages of very long hours, disappointment, disillusionment, self-doubt and reduced self-esteem. However, after a number of years of continuing dedication, a relentless can-do attitude and a growing self-confidence, their efforts started to show results. Things became easier as time rolled on. It was just like that for me too and I would suggest that these stages are experienced by the majority of people who decide to plough their own furrow in life. Great success lies in wait for those with a propensity for taking calculated risks and also showing persistency and patience.

I have mentioned that I have been helped enormously over the years by other, more experienced, people who were further along the road than I was. They often reached down the ladder to help me up and, by the natural law of reciprocity, I have been keen to do likewise with those who need my help. I am a great believer in what goes around comes around.

The bare fact is that, like most people, I am nothing special. I don't feel that I have been endowed with any exceptional talent or ability save perhaps a determination to work really hard and to keep on trying when others may have given up. I once overheard someone say of me, "He'll never set the world alight. He's one of life's plodders". Actually, setting the world alight never appealed to me anyway. I personally feel that there's an awful lot of benefit to be gained from plodding (Think about the extraordinary efforts of the late Captain Tom). So long as the end result of one's effort is something which is beneficial to oneself and others, there's an awful lot to be said for plodding. That's how horses plough fields.

The most extraordinary results can be achieved over a period of time if you just keep on doing what you enjoy for long enough. Do it bit-by-bit, little-by-little, inch-by-inch or yes, you've guessed it ... ONE SPOONFUL AT A TIME!

"A little progress
each day
adds up
to big results".

(Unknown)

www.ingramcontent.com/pod-product-compliance
Lightning Source LLC
Chambersburg PA
CBHW071623080526
44588CB00010B/1244